BOOKENDS

BOOKENDS

Collected Intros and Outros

MICHAEL CHABON

HARPER PERENNIAL

NEW YORK • LONDON • TORONTO • SYDNEY • NEW DELHI • AUCKLAND

HARPER ● PERENNIAL

FIRST HARPER PERENNIAL PAPERBACK EDITION PUBLISHED 2019.

Designed by Jamie Lynn Kerner

Library of Congress Cataloging-in-Publication Data has been applied for.

ISBN 978-0-06-285129-1 (pbk.)

19 20 21 22 23   LSC   10 9 8 7 6 5 4 3 2 1

To Jennifer Barth

I remind you that all things are but a beginning, forever beginning.
—ST. ALIA OF THE KNIFE

Contents

OUTROS

APPENDIX: LINER NOTES

Meta-Introduction

"I NEVER READ INTRODUCTIONS," SAYS ROSE, THE YOUNGER OF my two daughters. She thinks it over for a second, frowns; the statement doesn't quite ring true. She emends it: "Well, I've read *two*," she says. One turns out to be Jack Kerouac's introduction to Robert Frank's *The Americans*, required reading for a photography class: "But it was fine because I like his style." The other is Sherman Alexie's introduction to his own *The Lone Ranger and Tonto Fistfight in Heaven* (a favorite book, and author, of Rose's), because "it felt like it would be rude not to."

I suspect that my daughter's antipathy toward introductions (we did not discuss postscripts) is fairly common among avid readers. People who never bother to read what is more properly styled a *foreword* (in which one writer presents the work of another) or a *preface* (in which the writer herself, often retrospectively, reflects on her own work) are likely as numerous as people who don't bother with user manuals before launching the software application or powering up the widget.

You will not find me among either group; in the first instance out of hard experience but in the second out of love, pure love, from the time of my first encounter, circa 1979, with John Cheever's all-too-brief preface to his *Stories*, which contains the following passage, in which I now detect a premonitory stirring, two decades ahead of schedule, of *The Amazing Adventures of Kavalier & Clay*:

> These stories seem at times to be stories of a long-lost world
> when the city of New York was still filled with a river light,
> when you heard the Benny Goodman quartets from a radio in
> the corner stationery store, and when almost everybody wore
> a hat.

Certain forewords—Susan Sontag's to *The Barthes Reader*, Walter Benjamin's to *Fables of Leskov*—and prefaces—Raymond Chandler's to *The Simple Art of Murder*, Robert Towne's to the published script of *Chinatown*, Elmore Leonard's to his *Complete Western Stories*—have become beloved, even crucial texts for me, to be regularly re-read—as are Nabokov's afterword to *Lolita* and Leigh Brackett's to her *Best of* collection.

Some forewords are *transitive*: acts of seduction that are at the same time documents of earlier seductions. I already had a serious literary crush on Susan Sontag when I saw her name on the cover of *The Barthes Reader* and plunged into her foreword, at which point I discovered that Sontag, in turn, had a serious literary crush on this droll-looking Frenchman in his ubiquitous cardigan; I emerged from her foreword with a crush of my own on the late M. Barthes. Other forewords are *parasitical*; like cuckoos' eggs laid in crows' nests they hatch and flourish at the expense of their hosts. The fables of Nikolai Leskov are fine, if you like that sort of thing, but I can't imagine life without "The Storyteller," Benjamin's preface to a German translation of that Russian classic. Benjamin's diamantine epigrammatic style is on dazzling display throughout the piece but in no other writing of his does it do the work of heartbreak so powerfully as toward the end of the first section of "The Storyteller," where Benjamin collapses all the industrialized brutality and disruption of the First World War into some fifty words:

> A generation that had gone to school on a horse-drawn streetcar now stood under the open sky in a countryside in which nothing remained unchanged but the clouds, and beneath these clouds, in a field of force of destructive torrents and explosions, was the tiny, fragile human body.

But Benjamin's cuckoo's egg also had a lasting, personal effect on me, far more acute than anything I got from the *Fables* it nominally served to introduce. I used to worry, sometimes—in particular after I read Frank O'Connor's seminal meditation on the short story, *The Lonely Voice*—that unlike James Joyce, Anton Chekhov, A. E. Coppard, and the other writers Frank O'Connor lionized in *The Lonely Voice,* I was not really *from* anywhere. My family had been on the move for three generations or more, on both sides, and by the age of twenty-five I had lived in more than a dozen different places. The distinction Benjamin draws, in his foreword to Leskov, between storytellers who stay put and accumulate stockpiles of local lore and those who travel the world collecting the material of the tales they bring home, went a long way to reassuring me that my rootlessness was not only a legitimate condition for writing but, potentially, a theme worth exploring in my work.

As for prefaces (and afterwords), these may be explanatory, apologetic, triumphal, tendentious, rueful, score-settling, spiteful, bibliographic, theoretical (as is the case with Chandler's), or gently

embarrassed (as is the case with Cheever's) but the best of them—
like Cheever's—are also what I would call *restorative*. They unstop-
per the vial that contains, like some volatile oil, the fragrance of
the time in which the prefaced work was engendered, conceived,
or written, summoning for writer and reader alike a sensuous jolt
of things past: Cheever's Goodman-haunted stationery stores; the
motels and dusty mountainsides of Nabokov's midcentury transcontinental butterfly hunt; Towne's ache for the smell of orange
groves and all the lost Los Angeles that it encodes; and the Malibu,
desolate and wild as Barsoom, of Leigh Brackett's girlhood.

There are many reasons a writer might agree to provide an introduction to her own or another writer's book: affection, gratitude,
regret, revenge, enthusiasm, a desire to evangelize or set the record
straight. I've done it for some of those reasons, and more. But the
primary motivation for writing introductions has been the same as
for everything I write: a hope of bringing pleasure to the reader—to
some reader, somewhere. In this hope my sole assurance has been
the pleasure I've taken as a reader, over the years, in the prefaces,
forewords, and afterwords—the intros and outros—written by
others. I'm aware that this assurance may be far from sufficient
for many readers, however, and I would encourage skippers of introductions to put this book down and seek pleasure elsewhere—
but what would be the point?

INTROS

The Wes Anderson Collection, Matt Zoller Seitz

T HE WORLD IS SO BIG, SO COMPLICATED, SO REPLETE WITH marvels and surprises that it takes years for most people to begin to notice that it is, also, irretrievably broken. We call this period of research "childhood."

There follows a program of renewed inquiry, often involuntary, into the nature and effects of mortality, entropy, heartbreak, violence, failure, cowardice, duplicity, cruelty, and grief; the researcher learns their histories, and their bitter lessons, by heart. Along the way, he or she discovers that the world has been broken for as long as anyone can remember, and struggles to reconcile this fact with the ache of cosmic nostalgia that arises, from time to time, in the researcher's heart: an intimation of vanished glory, of lost wholeness, a memory of the world unbroken. We call the moment at which this ache first arises "adolescence." The feeling haunts people all their lives.

Everyone, sooner or later, gets a thorough schooling in brokenness. The question becomes: what to do with the pieces? Some people hunker down atop the local pile of ruins and make do, Bedouins tending their goats in the shade of shattered giants. Others set about breaking what remains of the world into bits ever smaller and more jagged, kicking through the rubble like kids running through piles of leaves. And some people, passing among the scattered pieces of that great overturned jigsaw puzzle, start to pick up a piece here, a piece there, with a vague yet irresistible notion that perhaps something might be done about putting the thing back together again.

Two difficulties with this latter scheme at once present themselves. First of all, we have only ever glimpsed, as if through half-closed lids, the picture on the lid of the jigsaw-puzzle box. Second, no matter how diligent we have been about picking up pieces along the way, we will never have anywhere near enough of them to finish the job. The most we can hope to accomplish with our handful of salvaged bits—the bittersweet harvest of observation and experience—is to build a little world of our own. A scale model of that mysterious original, unbroken, half-remembered. Of course, the worlds we build out of our store of fragments can only be approximations, partial and inaccurate. As representations of the vanished whole that haunts us, they must be accounted failures. And yet in that very failure, in their gaps and inaccuracies, they may yet be faithful maps, accurate scale models, of this beautiful and broken world. We call these scale models "works of art."

In their set design and camerawork, their use of stop-motion, maps, and models, Wes Anderson's films readily, even eagerly, concede the "miniature" quality of the worlds he builds. And yet these worlds span continents and decades. They comprise crime, adultery, brutality, suicide, the death of a parent, the drowning of a child, moments of profound joy and transcendence. Vladimir

Nabokov, his life cleaved by exile, created a miniature version of
the homeland he would never see again and tucked it, with a jew-
eler's precision, into the housing of John Shade's miniature epic of
family sorrow. Anderson—who has suggested that the breakup of
his parents' marriage was a defining experience of his life—adopts
a Nabokovian procedure with the families or quasi-families at the
heart of all his films, from *Rushmore* forward, creating a series of
scale-model households that, like the Zemblas and Estotilands and
other lost "kingdoms by the sea" in Nabokov, intensify our experience of brokenness and loss by compressing them. That is the
paradoxical power of the scale model; a child holding a globe has
a more direct, more intuitive grasp of the earth's scope and vari-
ety, of its local vastness and its cosmic tininess, than a man who
spends a year in circumnavigation. Grief, at full-scale, is too big
for us to take in; it literally cannot be comprehended. Anderson,
like Nabokov, understands that distance can increase our understanding of grief, allowing us to see it whole. But distance does
not—ought not—necessarily imply a withdrawal. In order to gain
sufficient perspective on the pain of exile and the murder of his father, Nabokov did not, in writing *Pale Fire,* step back from them. He
reduced their scale, and let his patience, his precision, his mastery
of detail—detail, the god of the model-maker—do the rest. With
each of his films, Anderson's total command of detail—both the
physical detail of his sets and costumes, and the emotional detail of
the uniformly beautiful performances he elicits from his actors—
has enabled him to increase the persuasiveness of his own family Zemblas, without sacrificing any of the paradoxical emotional
power that distance affords.

  Anderson's films have frequently been compared to the boxed
assemblages of Joseph Cornell's, and it's a useful comparison, as
long as one bears in mind that the crucial element, in a Cornell

box, is neither the imagery and objects it deploys, nor the romantic narratives it incorporates and undermines, nor the playfulness and precision with which its objects and narratives have been arranged. The important thing, in a Cornell box, is the *box*.

Cornell always took pains to construct his boxes himself; indeed the box is the only part of a Cornell work literally "made" by the artist. The box, to Cornell, is a *gesture*—it draws a boundary around the things it contains, and forces them into a defined relationship, not merely with each other, but with everything on the far side of the box. The box sets out the scale of a ratio, it mediates the halves of a metaphor. It makes explicit, in plain, handcrafted wood and glass, the yearning of a model-maker to analogize the world, and at the same time it frankly emphasizes the limitations, the confines, of his or her ability to do so.

The things in Anderson's films that recall Cornell's boxes— the strict, steady, four-square construction of individual shots, by which the cinematic frame becomes a Cornellian gesture, a box drawn around the world of the film; the teeming, gridded, curio-cabinet sets at the heart of *Life Aquatic, Darjeeling*, and *Mr. Fox*—are often cited as evidence of his work's "artificiality," at times with the implication, simple-minded and profoundly mistaken, that a high degree of artifice is somehow inimical to seriousness, to honest emotion, to so-called authenticity. All movies, of course, are equally artificial; it's just that some are more honest about it than others. In this important sense, the hand-built, model-kit artifice on display behind the pane of an Anderson box is a *guarantor* of authenticity; indeed, I would argue that artifice, openly expressed, is the only true "authenticity" an artist can lay claim to.

Anderson's films, like the boxes of Cornell, or the novels of Nabokov, understand and demonstrate that the magic of art, which renders beauty out of brokenness, disappointment, failure, decay, even ugliness and violence—is authentic only to the degree that it attempts to conceal neither the bleak facts nor the tricks employed in pulling off the presto chango. It is honest only to the degree that it builds its precise and inescapable box around its maker's $x{:}y$-scale version of the world.

"For my next trick," says Joseph Cornell, or Vladimir Nabokov, or Wes Anderson, "I have put the world into a box." And when he opens the box, you see something dark and glittering, an orderly mess of shards, refuse, bits of junk and feather and butterfly wing, tokens and totems of memory, maps of exile, documentation of loss. And you say, leaning in, "The world!" (2013)

Trickster Makes This World, Lewis Hyde

A BOOK IS A MAP; THE TERRITORY IT CHARTS MAY BE "THE world," or other books, or the mind of the cartographer. A great book maps all three territories at once, or rather persuades us that they—world, literature, and a single human imagination—are co-extensive. Of course that isn't true. A map, like all abstractions, is a kind of lie. The world outside our heads, and the world inside them, and the lines by which we represent inside and out, do not really correspond, any more than do a squirt of stars, a connect-the-dot plan of the constellations, and the tendency of our minds to see, in an apparent arc of stars, two fish struggling on a line.

A great book, therefore, is in part an act of deception, a tissue of lies: a trick. Indeed, it plays the fundamental human trick of finding, or discovering, or imposing meaning in the senseless, pattern in chaos, fish and princesses and monsters in the heavens. That act of deception is at root a self-deception, conscious and unconscious, and without it life would be—life *is*—a terrible, useless procedure bracketed by orgasm and putrefaction. Small wonder that we should have come, therefore, to revere the One who perpetrates that lie, who embodies the contingent and in so doing lends it the appearance of necessity. His name is Trickster. And *this* great book, by Lewis Hyde, is a map of Trickster's wanderings through literature, human history, and the rich, surprising territory of Hyde's mind. I have never found a map whose reckoning, however tricksy, felt more true.

We have at various moments in our history of foolishness persuaded ourselves that we have outgrown mythology, found clever, distancing ways to package it, to handle it with the tools of irony or scholarship or literary effect, to reduce it to fairy tale, ornamentation, motif. We have, alternatively but with as little sense, sought to view the myths of our ancestors as a kind of secret key or users manual, a shortcut to the primal, the primitive, the natural, the repressed. I have been a lover of mythology all my life and both kinds of fool at various times, whether as a reader of Marvel's *The Mighty Thor* or of Robert Graves's *The White Goddess*. But in the end, in turns out, a myth is only a story, and a story is all we can count on for comfort here in this obscure and broken land between the first dazzle of consciousness and its final winking out. I am a mythophile by nature and a storyteller by profession, but before I read *Trickster Makes This World* I never truly understood that myths were only stories, and that stories were only lies, and that lies were all we had. In *Trickster Makes This World,* Hyde picks out one thread of ancient story and traces it, without post-Freudian archness or the sounding of Wiccan drums, across all its knots and frayings, from prehistory to Duchamp, from the escape narrative of Frederick Douglass to Hyde's own encounter with Coyote in the American southwest. In the resultant net of knotted story he catches us up like fish caught in a cord of stars.

My work as a writer and as an inheritor of the human bag of

lies has never quite recovered from the shock of my first encounter with *Trickster Makes This World*, which was only, in the end, an encounter with everything I already knew and had long possessed. It is in the way of confidence men and tricksters to sell you what you already own; but a great writer, in so doing, always finds a way to enrich you by the game. Before I read *Trickster* I felt lost among the territories of "genre" and "literary" fiction, wanting both to exalt and to entertain readers, to write like Marcel Proust *and* Robert E. Howard (multiplicands whose product may in fact be William Faulkner). I felt drawn to many paths at once, reeling blindfolded across the map of literature like a man seeking a piñata with a stick. After I read *Trickster Makes This World* I was not a bit less lost; I was still, like Trickster and all my fellow humans, trapped among the worlds, with, as one of our greatest Tricksters once put it, "No direction home." But now I knew, and have since never forgotten, that I was *born* to wander along the borderlands. To err—that is, to wander—is human. And so is the act of making a story out of our purposeless wanderings, as if they mattered, as if they had a beginning, a middle, and an end. They don't, but there is neither joy nor art nor pleasure to be made from saying so. Coyote wouldn't waste his time on a paltry truth like that. (2010)

The Long Ships, Frans G. Bengtsson

Iɴ ᴍʏ ᴄᴀʀᴇᴇʀ ᴀs ᴀ ʀᴇᴀᴅᴇʀ I ʜᴀᴠᴇ ᴇɴᴄᴏᴜɴᴛᴇʀᴇᴅ ᴏɴʟʏ three people who knew *The Long Ships*, and all of them, like me, loved it immoderately. Four for four: from this tiny but irrefutable sample I dare to extrapolate that this novel, first published in Sweden during the Second World War, stands ready, given the chance, to bring lasting pleasure to every single human being on the face of the earth.

The record of a series of three imaginary but plausible voyages (interrupted by a singularly eventful interlude of hanging around the house) undertaken by a crafty, resourceful, unsentimental, and mildly hypochondriacal Norseman named "Red Orm" Tosteson, *The Long Ships* is itself a kind of novelistic *Argos* aboard which, like the heroes of a great age, all the strategies deployed by European novelists over the course of the preceding century are united—if not for the first, then perhaps for the very last time. The Dioscuri of nineteenth-century Realism, factual precision and mundane detail, set sail on *The Long Ships* with nationalism, medievalism, and exoticism for shipmates, brandishing a banner of nineteenth-century Romance; but among the heroic crew mustered by Frans Bengtsson in his only work of fiction are an irony as harsh and forgiving as anything in Dickens, a wit and skepticism worthy of Stendhal, an epic Tolstoyan sense of the anti-epic, and the Herculean narrative drive, mighty and nimble, of Alexander Dumas. Like half the great European novels it is big, bloody, and far-ranging, concerned with war and treasure and the grand deeds of men and kings; like the other half it is intimate and domestic, centered firmly around the seasons and pursuits of village and farm, around weddings and births, around the hearths of women who see only too keenly through the grand pretensions of men and bloody kings.

It offers, therefore—as you might expect from a novel with the potential to please every literate human being in the entire world—something for everyone, and if until now *The Long Ships* has languished in the secondhand bins of the English-speaking world, this is certainly through no fault of its author, Frans Bengtsson, whom the reader comes to regard—as we come to regard any reliable, capable, and congenial companion in the course of any great novel, adventure, or novel of adventure—as a friend for life. Bengtsson re-creates the world of AD 1000, as seen through the eyes of some of its northernmost residents, with telling detail and persuasive historiography, with a keen grasp of the eternal bits that pebble the record of human vanity, and with the unflagging verve of a born storyteller—but above all, and this is the most remarkable of the book's many virtues, with an intimate detachment, a neighborly distance, a sincere irony, that feels at once ancient and postmodern. It is this astringent tone, undeceived, versed in human folly, at once charitable and cruel, that is the source of the novel's unique flavor, the poker-faced humor that is most beloved by those who love this book. Though at times the story, published in two parts each consisting of two parts over a span of several years, has an episodic feel, each of its individual components' narratives is well-constructed of the soundest timbers of epic, folktale, and ripping yarn, and as its hero grows old and sees his age passing away, that episodic quality comes to feel, in the end, not like some congeries of saga and tall tale but like the accurate representation of one long and crowded human life.

Nor can blame for the neglect of *The Long Ships* be laid at the feet of Bengtsson's English translator, Michael Meyer, who produced a version of the original the faithfulness of which I leave for the judgment of others, but whose utter deliciousness, as English, I readily proclaim. The antique chiming that stirs the air of the novel's sentences (without ever overpowering or choking that air with antique dust) recalls the epics and chronicles and history of our mother tongue (a history after all shared, up to a point, with the original Swedish), and the setting of parts of the action in Dark-Ages Britain further strengthens the reader's deceptive sense that he or she is, thanks to the translator's magic and art, reading a work of English literature. Toss in the novel's unceasing playfulness around the subject of Christianity and its relative virtues and shortcomings when compared to Islam, and, especially, to the Old Religion of the northern forests (a playfulness that cannot disguise the author's profound but lightly worn concern with questions of ethics and the right use and purpose of a life), and the startling presence, in a Swedish Viking story, of a sympathetic Jewish character, and you have a work whose virtues and surprises ought long since have given it a prominent place, at least, in the pantheon of the world's adventure literature if not world literature full stop.

The fault, therefore, must lie with the world, which, as any reader of *The Long Ships* could tell you, buries its treasures, despises its glories, and seeks contentment most readily in the places where it is least likely to be found. Fortunately for us, it is in just those unlikely places, as Red Orm quickly learns, that the opportunities and treasures of the world may often be found. My encounter with *The Long Ships* came when I was fourteen or fifteen, through the agency of a true adventurer, my mother's sister, Gail Cohen. Toward the end of the sixties she had set off, with the rest of her restless generation of psychic Vikings, on a journey that led from suburban Maryland, to California where she met and fell in love with a roving young Dane, to Denmark itself, where she settled and lived for twenty years. It was on one of her periodic visits home that she handed me a UK paperback edition of the book, published by Fontana, which she had randomly purchased at the airport in Copenhagen, partly because it was set in her adopted homeland, and partly because there was nothing on the rack that looked any better. "It's *really* good," she assured me, and I would soon discover for myself the truth of this assessment, which in turn I would repeat to other lucky people over the years to come. Gail's own adventure came to an end at home, in America, in the toils of cancer. When she looked back at the map of it, like most true adventurers, she saw moments of joy, glints of gold, and happy chances like the one that brought this book into her hands. But I fear that like most true adventurers—but unlike Bengtsson's congenitally fortunate hero— she also saw, looking back, that grief overtopped joy, that trash obscured the treasure, that, in the end, the bad luck outweighed the good.

That is the great advantage, of course, that reading holds over what we call "real life." Adventure is a dish that is best eaten takeout, in the comfort of one's own home. As you begin your meal, as you set off with Frans Bengtsson and Red Orm and the restless spirit of my aunt, I salute you, and bid you farewell, and even though I have just finished reading the book for the fourth time, I envy you the pleasure you are about to find in the pages of *The Long Ships*. When you arrive at its bittersweet, but mostly sweet, conclusion, I trust that you will turn to your shipmate, your companion in adventure, and swear by ancient oaths, as I hereby swear to you: It is *really* good. (2010)

Secret Skin
An Essay in Unitard Theory

THE DANGER OF THE CAPE

WHEN I WAS A BOY, I HAD A RELIGIOUS-SCHOOL TEACHER named Mr. Spector whose job was to confront us with the peril we presented to ourselves. Jewish Ethics was the name of the class. We must have been eight or nine.

Mr. Spector used a workbook to guide the discussion; every Sunday, we began by reading a kind of modern parable or cautionary tale, and then contended with a series of imponderable questions. One day, for example, we discussed the temptations of shoplifting; another class was devoted to all the harm to oneself and to others that could be caused by the telling of lies. Mr. Spector was a gently acerbic young man with a black beard and black Roentgen-ray eyes. He seemed to take our moral failings for granted and, perhaps as a result, favored lively argument over reproach or condemnation. I enjoyed our discussions, while remaining perfectly aloof at my core from the issues they raised. I was, at the time, an awful liar, and quite a few times had stolen chewing gum and baseball cards from the neighborhood Wawa. None of that seemed to have anything to do with Mr. Spector or the cases we studied in Jewish Ethics. All nine-year-olds are sophists and hypocrites; I found it no more difficult than any other kid to withhold my own conduct from consideration in passing measured judgment on the human race.

The one time I felt my soul to be in danger was the Sunday Mr. Spector raised the ethical problem of escapism, particularly as it was experienced in the form of comic books. That day, we started off with a fine story about a boy who loved Superman so much that he tied a red towel around his neck, climbed up to the roof of his house, and, with a cry of "Up, up, and away," leaped to his death. There was known to have been such a boy, Mr. Spector informed us—at least one verifiable boy, so enraptured and so betrayed by the false dream of Superman that it killed him.

The explicit lesson of the story was that what was found between the covers of a comic book was fantasy, and "fantasy" meant pretty lies, the consumption of which failed to prepare you for what lay outside those covers. Fantasy rendered you unfit to face "reality" and its hard pavement. Fantasy betrayed you, and thus, by implication, your wishes, your dreams and longings, everything you carried around inside your head that only you and Superman and Elliot S! Maggin could understand—all these would betray you, too. There were ancillary arguments to be made as well, about the culpability of those who produced such fare, sold it to minors, or permitted their children to bring it into the house.

These arguments were mostly lost on me, a boy who consumed a dozen comic books a week, all of them cheerfully provided to him by his (apparently iniquitous) father. Sure, I might not be prepared for reality—point granted—but, on the other hand, if I ever found myself in the Bottle City of Kandor, under the bell jar in the Fortress of Solitude, I would know not to confuse Superman's Kryptonian double (Van-Zee) with Clark Kent's (Vol-Don). Rather, what struck me, with the force of a blow, was recognition, a profound moral recognition of the implicit, indeed the secret, premise of the behavior of the boy on the roof. For that fool of a boy had not been doomed by the deceitful power of comic books, which after all were only bundles of paper, staples, and ink, and couldn't hurt anybody. That boy had been killed by the irresistible syllogism of Superman's cape.

One knew, of course, that it was not the red cape any more than it was the boots, the tights, the trunks, or the trademark "S" that gave Superman the ability to fly. That ability derived from the effects of the rays of our yellow sun on Superman's alien anatomy, which had evolved under the red sun of Krypton. And yet you had only to tie a towel around your shoulders to feel the strange vibratory pulse of flight stirring in the red sun of your heart.

I, too, had climbed to a dangerous height, with my face to the breeze, and felt magically alone of my kind. I had imagined the streak of my passage like a red-and-blue smear on the windowpane of vision. I had been Batman, too, and the Mighty Thor. I had stood cloaked in the existential agonies of the Vision, son of a robot and grandson of a lord of the ants. A few years after that Sunday in Mr. Spector's class, at the pinnacle of my career as a hero of the imagination, I briefly transformed myself (more about this later) into a superpowered warrior-knight known as Aztec. And all that I needed to effect the change was to fasten a terry-cloth beach towel around my neck.

THE SECRET ORIGIN OF UNITARD THEORY

IT WAS NOT ABOUT ESCAPE, I WANTED TO TELL MR. SPECTOR, thus unwittingly plagiarizing in advance the well-known formula of a (fictitious) pioneer and theorist of superhero comics, Sam Clay. It was about *transformation*.

AND THE SECRET ANXIETY OF ORIGIN

IT IS COMMONPLACE TO ASSERT THE HERITAGE OF THE COS-tumed heroes of comic books in the misty mythosphere of the ancient world, and it's tempting to view accounts of superhero or-igins, the sine qua non of the superhero narrative, as proof of that legendary inheritance. Hyperbolic myths of origin have from the mistiest times served to lend a paradoxical plausibility to the biog-raphies of heroes. Baskets found floating in the bulrushes, oracle-doomed infants abandoned on hillsides, babies born with hammers in their hands. Traditional origin myths affirm the constant, even prenatal, presence of the marvelous in the hero's life, of a vein of wonder that marbles it from one end to the other like the words embedded in a stick of Brighton rock.

But apart from a marked tendency to orphanhood, the super-hero generally disappoints the expectations of mythology. The cos-tumed hero—if not a mutant—is born powerless and unheralded like the rest of us. It takes the bite of a radioactive spider, or some other form of half-disaster (a lab explosion, a brutal act of street violence, a secret government experiment, an emergency transfu-sion of mongoose blood) to give birth to the hero, who then springs, full-grown like Athena, from the prised-open cranium of everyday life. The superhero works long hours at a day job (even that playboy Bruce Wayne puts in an awful lot of time at the office) and struggles in every way—legally, socially, emotionally—to fit in to the expectations of the quotidian world. The superhero in general has no overt or obligatory sense of destiny, none of the lust for glory and fame and treasure that characterize the classical hero. Superheroes spend a lot of time wishing they could just stay home, spend time with their families and loved ones, date the girl they love, be like everybody else. They excel because they cannot help it, or because it would be wrong not to, or because they need to prove their worth, or to exonerate themselves, or to repay the debt they feel to society, their parents, the wizard in a subway tunnel who endowed them with magic might. Above all, superheroes have secret identities; they have lives and natures that their pursuit of heroism obliges them to conceal, to downplay, to deny. They cannot engage in the boastful trumpeting of one's name and parentage so beloved among traditional heroes.

It is for this reason, and not out of their legendary heritage in the mythosphere, that comic books, the bastard child of newspaper strips and pulp magazines, have always displayed an arriviste fixation on questions and mysteries of origin. The superhero is a parvenu in the house of adventure, an immigrant on the shores of myth.

This general fixation with the origin story goes beyond the particulars of Kryptonian birth or gamma-ray exposure to encompass the origin of the idea of the costumed superhero itself. Fans and historians of comic books (those synonymous creatures) have devoted loving years and pages in the thousands to isolating with some kind of precision the moment and the conditions that led to the birth of the costumed hero. And when they faltered in their efforts, in have strode the psychologists, the critics, the analysts, and, with mixed results, the comic book writers and artists themselves.

The comic book preexisted the superhero, but so barely and with so little distinction that the medium has seemed indistinguishable in the cultural mind from its first stroke of brilliance. There were costumed crime fighters before Superman (the Phantom, Zorro), but only as there were pop quartets before the Beatles. Superman invented and exhausted his genre in a single bound. All the tropes, all the clichés and conventions, all the possibilities, all the longings and wishes and neuroses that have driven and fed and burdened the superhero comic over the past seventy years were implied by and contained within that little red rocket ship hurtling toward Earth. That moment—Krypton exploding, *Action Comics* #1—is generally seen to be Minute Zero of the superhero idea.

About the reasons for the arrival of Superman at that zero moment there is less agreement. In the theories of origin put forward by fans, critics, and other origin-obsessives, the *idea* of Superman has been accounted the offspring or recapitulation, in no particular order, of Frederic Nietzsche; of Philip Wylie (in his novel *Gladiator*); of the strengths, frailties, and neuroses of Jerry Siegel and Joe Shuster; of the aching wishfulness of the Great Depression; of the (Jewish) immigrant experience; of the mastermind stratagems of popular texts in their sinister quest for reader domination; of repressed Oedipal fantasies; of fascism; of capitalism; of the production modes of mass culture (and not in a good way); of celebrated strongmen and proponents of physical culture like Eugene Sandow; and of a host of literary not-quite-Supermans (chief among them Doc Savage) who preceded him.

Most of these rationales of origin depend, to some extent, on history; they index the advent of Superman in late 1938 to various intellectual, social, and economic trends of the Depression years, to the influence or aura of contemporary celebrities and authors, to the structure and demands of magazine publishing and distribution, et

cetera. To suit my purpose here I might construct a similar etiology
of the superhero costume, making due reference, say, to professional
wrestling and circus attire of the early twentieth century, to the
boots-cloak-and-tights ensembles worn by swashbucklers and cav-
aliers in stage plays and Hollywood films, to contemporary men's
athletic wear with its unitard construction and belted trunks, to the
designs of Alex Raymond and Hal Foster and the amazing pulp-
magazine cover artist Frank R. Paul. I could cite the influence of
Deco and Streamline design aesthetics, with their roots in fantasies
of power, speed, and flight, or posit the costume as a kind of fashion
alter ego of the heavy, boxy profile of men's clothing at the time.

Thus, while claiming, on the one hand, a dubiously ahistorical,
archetypical source for the superhero idea in the Jungian vastness
of legend, we dissolve its true universality in a foaming bath of pe-
riodized explanations, and render the superhero and his costume a
time-fixed idea that is always already going out of fashion. When
in fact the point of origin is not a date or a theory or a conjunction
of cultural trends but a story, the intersection of a wish and the tip
of a pencil.

A FAITHFUL SCALE MODEL OF NOTHING

NOW THE TIME HAS COME TO PROPOSE, OR CONFRONT, A FUN-
damental truth: like the being who wears it, the superhero costume
is, by definition, an impossible object. It cannot exist. One may
easily find suggestive evidence for this assertion at any large comic
book convention by studying the spectacle of the brave and bold
convention attendees, those members of the general comics-fan
public who show up in costume and go shpatziring around the
ballrooms and exhibition halls dressed as Wolverine, say, or the

Joker's main squeeze, Harley Quinn. Without exception, even the most splendid of these getups is at best a disappointment. Every seam, every cobweb strand of duct-tape gum, every laddered fishnet stocking or visible ridge of underpants elastic—every stray mark, pulled thread, speck of dust—acts to spoil what is instantly revealed to have been, all along, an illusion.

The appearance of realism in a superhero costume made from real materials is generally recognized to be difficult to pull off, and many such costumes do not even bother to simulate the presumable effect on the eye and the spirit of the beholder were Black Bolt to stride, trailing a positronic lace of Kirby crackle, into a ballroom of the Overland Park Marriott. This disappointing air of saggy trouser seats, bunchy underarms, and wobbly shoulder vanes may be the result of imaginative indolence, the sort that would permit a grown man to tell himself he will find gratification in walking the exhibition floor wearing a pair of Dockers, a Jägermeister hoodie, and a rubber Venom mask complete with punched-out eyeholes and a flopping rubber bockwurst of a tongue.

But realism is not, in fact, merely *difficult*; it is hopeless. A plausibly heroic physique is of no avail in this regard, nor is even the most fervent willingness to believe in oneself as the man or woman in the cape. Even those costumed conventioneers who go all out, working year-round to amass, scrounge, or counterfeit cleverly the materials required to put together, with glue gun, soldering iron, makeup, and needle and thread, a faithful and accurate Black Canary or Ant-Man costume, find themselves prey to forces, implacable as gravity, of tawdriness, gimcrackery, and unwitting self-ridicule. And in the end they look no more like Black Canary or Ant-Man than does the poor zhlub in the Venom mask with a three-day pass hanging around his neck on a lanyard.

This sad outcome even in the wake of thousands of dollars

spent and months of hard work given to sewing and to packing foam rubber into helmets has an obvious, an unavoidable, explanation: a superhero's costume is constructed not of fabric, foam rubber, or adamantium but of halftone dots, Pantone color values, inked containment lines, and all the cartoonist's sleight of hand. The superhero costume as drawn disdains the customary relationship in the fashion world between sketch and garment. It makes no suggestions. It has no agenda. Above all, it is not waiting to find fulfillment as cloth draped on a body. A constructed superhero costume is a replica with no original, a model built on a scale of x:1. However accurate and detailed, such a work has the tidy airlessness of a model-train layout but none of the gravitas that little railyards and townscapes derive from making faithful reference to homely things. The graphic purity of the superhero costume means that the more effort and money you lavish on fine textiles, metal grommets, and leather trim the deeper your costume will be sucked into the silliness singularity that swallowed, for example, Joel Schumacher's Batman and Robin and their four nipples.

In fact, the most reliable proof of the preposterousness of superhero attire whenever it is translated, as if by a Kugelmass device, from the pages of comics to the so-called real world can be found in film and television adaptations of superhero characters. George Reeves's stodgy pajamas-like affair in the old *Superman* TV series and Adam West's mod doll clothes in *Batman* have lately given way to purportedly more "realistic" versions in rubber, leather, and plastic—pseudo-utilitarian coveralls that draw inspiration in equal measure from spacesuits, catsuits, and scuba suits, and from (one presumes) regard for the dignity of actors who have seen the old George Reeves and Adam West shows and would not be caught dead in those glorified Underoos. In its attempts to slip the confines of the paneled page, the superhero costume betrays its nonexistence, like one of those deep-sea creatures that evolved to thrive in the crushing darkness of the seabed so that when you haul them up to the dazzling surface they burst.

One might go further and argue not only that the superhero costume has (and needs) no referent in the world of textiles and latex, but also that, even within its own proper comic book context, it can be said not to exist, not to want to exist—can be said to advertise, even to revel in, its own notional status. This illusionary quality of the drawn costume can readily be seen if we attempt to delimit the elements of the superhero wardrobe, to inventory its minimum or requisite components.

THE SILVER GLUTEAL CLEFT OF THE SPACEWAYS

WE CAN START BY THROWING AWAY OUR MASKS. SUPERMAN, arguably the first and the greatest of all costumed heroes, has never bothered with one, nor have Captain Marvel, Luke Cage, Wonder Woman, Valkyrie, and Supergirl. All those individuals, like many of their peers (Hawkman, Giant-Man), also go around barehanded, which suggests that we can safely dispense with our gauntlets (whether finned, rolled, or worn with a jaunty slash at the cuff). Capes have been an object of scorn among discerning superheroes at least since 1974, when Captain America, having abandoned his old career in protest over Watergate, briefly took on the nom de guerre Nomad, dressed himself in a piratical ensemble of midnight blue and gold, and brought his first exploit as a stateless hero to an inglorious end by tripping over his own flowing cloak.

So let's lose the cape. As for the boots—we are not married to the boots. After all, Iron Fist sports a pair of kung-fu slippers, the Spirit wears brown brogues, Zatanna works her magic in stiletto heels, and Beast, Ka-Zar, and Mantis wear no shoes at all. Perhaps, though, we had better hold on to our unitards, crafted of some nameless but readily available fabric that, like a thin matte layer, at once coats and divulges the splendor of our musculature. Assemble the collective, all-time memberships of the Justice League of America, the Justice Society of America, the Avengers, the Defenders, the Invaders, the X-Men, and the Legion of Super-Heroes (and let us not forget the Legion of Substitute Heroes), and you will probably find that almost all of them, from Nighthawk to the Chlorophyll Kid, arrive wearing some version of the classic leotard-tights ensemble. And yet—not everyone. Not Wonder Woman, in her star-spangled hot pants and eagle bustier; not the Incredible Hulk or Martian Manhunter or the Sub-Mariner.

Consideration of the last named leads us to cast a critical eye, finally, on our little swim trunks, typically worn with a belt, pioneered by Kit Walker, the Phantom of the old newspaper strip, and popularized by the super-trendsetter of Metropolis. The Sub-Mariner wears nothing *but* a Eurotrashy green Speedo, suggesting that, at least by the decency standards of the old Comics Code, this minimal garment marks the zero degree of superheroic attire. And yet, of course, the Flash, Green Lantern, and many others make do without trunks over their tights; the forgoing of trunks in favor of a continuous flow of fabric from legs to torso is frequently employed to lend a suggestion of speed, sleekness, a kind of uncluttered modernism. And the Hulk never goes around in anything but those tattered purple trousers.

So we are left with, literally, nothing at all: the human form, unadorned, smooth, muscled, and ready, let's say, to sail the starry ocean of the cosmos on the deck of a gleaming surfboard. A naked spacefarer, sheathed in a silvery pseudoskin that affords all the protection one needs from radiation and cosmic dust while meeting

Code standards by neatly neutering one, the shining void between the legs serving to signify that one is not (as one often appears to be when seen from behind) naked as an interstellar jaybird.

Here is a central paradox of superhero attire: from panther black to lantern green, from the faintly Hapsburg pomp of the fifties-era Legion of Super-Heroes costumes to the "Mad Max" space grunge of Lobo, from sexy fishnet to vibranium—for all the mad recombinant play of color, style, and materials that the superhero costume makes with its limited number of standard components, it ultimately takes its deepest meaning and serves its primary function in the depiction of the naked human form, unfettered, perfect, and free. The superheroic wardrobe resembles a wildly permutated alphabet of ideograms conceived only to express the eloquent power of silence.

GOTHAM IS BURNING

A PUBLIC AMNESIA, AN AVOWED LACK OF HISTORY, IS THE STANdard pretense of the costumed superhero. From the point of view of the man or woman or child in the street, gaping up at the sky and skyscrapers, the appearance of a new hero over Metropolis or New York or Astro City is always a matter of perfect astonishment. There have been no portents or warnings, and afterward one never learns anything new or gains any explanations.

The story of a superhero's origin must be kept secret, occulted as rigorously from public knowledge as the alter ego, as if it were a source of shame. Superman conceals, archived in the Fortress of Solitude and accessible only to him, not only his own history—the facts and tokens of his birth and arrival on Earth, of his Smallville childhood, of his exploits and adventures—but the history of his

Kryptonian family and, indeed, of his entire race. Batman similarly hides his story and its proofs in the trophy chambers of the Batcave.

In theory, the costume forms part of the strategy of conceal-ment. But in fact the superhero's costume often functions as a kind of magic screen onto which the repressed narrative may be pro-jected. No matter how well he or she hides its traces, the secret narrative of transformation, of rebirth, is given up by the costume. Sometimes this secret is betrayed through the allusion of style or form: Robin's gaudy uniform hints at the murder of his circus-acrobat parents, Iron Man's at the flawed heart that requires a life-support device, which is the primary function of his armor.

More often, the secret narrative is hinted at with a kind of enigmatic, dreamlike obviousness right on the hero's chest or belt buckle, in the form of the requisite insignia. Superman's "S," we have been told, only coincidentally stands for Superman: in fact, the emblem is the coat of arms of the ancient Kryptonian House of El, from which he descends. A stylized bat alludes to the animal whose chance flight through a window sealed Bruce Wayne's fate; a lightning bolt encapsulates the secret history of Captain Marvel; an eight-legged glyph immortalizes the bug whose bite doomed Peter Parker to his glorious and woebegone career.

We say "secret identity" and adopt a series of cloaking strate-gies to preserve it, but what we are actually trying to conceal is a narrative: not who we are but the story of how we got that way—and, by implication, of all that we lacked, and all that we were not, before the spider bit us. Yet our costume conceals nothing, reveals everything: it is our secret skin, exposed and exposing us for all the world to see. Superheroism is a kind of transvestism; our superdrag serves at once to obscure the exterior self that no longer defines us while betraying, with half-unconscious panache, the truth of the story we carry in our hearts, the story of our transformation, of our story's recommencement, of our rebirth into the world of adventure, of story itself.

MY SECRET ORIGIN

I BECAME AZTEC IN THE SUMMER OF 1973, IN COLUMBIA, Maryland, a planned suburban utopia halfway between Smallville and Metropolis. It happened one summer day as I was walking to the swimming pool with a friend. He wore a pair of midnight-blue bathing trunks; my trunks were loud, with patches of pink, orange, gold, and brown overprinted with abstract patterns that we took for Aztec (though they were probably Polynesian). In those days, a pair of bathing trunks did not in the least resemble the baggy board shorts that boys and men wear swimming today. Ours were made of stretchy polyester double knit that came down the thigh just past the level of the crotch, and fashion fitted them with a sewn-on, false belt of elastic webbing that buckled at the front with a metal clasp. They looked, in other words, just like the trunks favored by costumed heroes ever since the last son of Krypton came voguing down the super-catwalk, back in 1938. Around our throats we knotted our beach towels (his was blue, mine a fine 1973 shade of burnt orange), those enchanted cloaks whose power Mr. Spector had failed to understand or to recall from his own childhood. They fluttered out behind us, catching the breeze from our imaginations, as Darklord and Aztec walked along.

Darklord carried a sword, and wore a Barbuta helmet, with a flowing crusader cloak and invulnerable chain mail of "lunar steel." Aztec wore tights and a feathered cloak and wielded a magic staff tipped with obsidian. We had begun the journey that day, through the street-melting, shimmering green Maryland summer morning,

as a pair of lonely boys with nothing in common but that loneliness, which we shared with Superman and Batman, who shared
it with each other—a fundamental loneliness and a wild aptitude
for transformation. But with every step we became Darklord and
Aztec a little more surely, a little more irrevocably, transformed by
the green-lantern rays of fancy, by the spider bite of inspiration, by
the story we were telling each other and ourselves about two costumed superheroes, about the new selves that had been revealed
by our secret skin.

Talking, retying the knots of our capes, flip-flops slapping
against the soles of our feet, we transformed not only ourselves. In
the space of that walk to the pool we also transformed the world,
shaping it into a place in which such things were possible: the rein-
carnation of an Arthurian knight could find solace and partnership
in the company of a latter-day Mesoamerican wizard. An entire
world of superheroic adventure could be dreamed up by a couple of
boys from Columbia, or Cleveland. And the self you knew you contained, the story you knew you had inside you, might find its way
like an emblem onto the spot right over your heart. All we needed
to do was accept the standing invitation that superhero comics ex-
tended to us by means of a towel. It was an invitation to enter into
the world of story, to join in the ongoing business of comic books,
and, with the knotting of a magical beach towel, to begin to wear
what we knew to be hidden inside us. (2008)

Julius Knipl, Real Estate Photographer, Ben Katchor

L IKE MANY PEOPLE, I WAS FIRST APPRISED OF THE WISTFUL and intrepid pilgrimage on which you are about to embark by Lawrence Weschler in his *New Yorker* profile of Ben Katchor, creator of the last great American comic strip.

It is a sad duty thus to anoint *Julius Knipl, Real Estate Photographer*. Perhaps no art form has ever flourished so brilliantly only to decline into such utter debasement, in such a brief period of time, as the newspaper strip. Reading the comics page in 1996, exactly one hundred years after the debut of Outcault's Yellow Kid, is, for those who still bother, half melancholy habit and half sentimental adherence to duty, a daily running up of a discredited flag in a forsaken outpost of an empire that collapsed.

Weschler's article dwelt at length, as do most commentators on Katchor, on the artist's preoccupation with the sensuous residuum of the past, those unexpected revelators of the all-but-forgotten, encountered in the stairwell of a hard-luck office building or on the dusty shelves of a decrepit pharmacy, those stray remnants of an earlier time that are hinted at in the surname of his protagonist, the stoop-shouldered wanderer, meditative soul, and former dance instructor Mr. Julius Knipl. And it is true that celebration of the chance survival, the memory wrapped like a knipl, or nest egg, in a beaded purse of forgetfulness, discovered in the back of a drawer, is the most immediately striking and perhaps the most accessible aspect of the strip. It was this aspect, initially, that led me to track down Katchor's first collection of strips, *Cheap Novelties*, and—the spell was on me now—to take out a subscription to *Forward*, currently the flagship paper of the scattershot and fluctuating Knipl syndicate. I'm a sucker, myself, for such chance survivals, because as I've confessed elsewhere I suffer intensely from bouts, at times almost disabling, of a limitless, all-encompassing nostalgia, extending well back into the years before I was born.

The mass synthesis, marketing, and distribution of versions and simulacrums of an artificial past, perfected over the last thirty years or so, has ruined the reputation and driven a fatal stake through the heart of nostalgia. Those of us who cannot make it from one end of a street to another without being momentarily upended by some fragment of outmoded typography, curve of chrome fender, or whiff of lavender hair oil from the pate of a semi-retired neighbor are compelled by the disrepute into which nostalgia has fallen to mourn secretly the passing of a million marvelous quotidian things.

The erasure of the past, and its replacement by animatronic replicas, politicians' narratives, and the fictions of advertisers, coupled with the explosive proliferation of new inventions and altered mores, ought to have produced a boom time for honest mourners of the vanished. Instead we find ourselves haunting the margins of a world loud with speculators in metal lunch boxes and Barbie dolls, postmodernists, and retro-rockers, quietly regretting the alternate chuckling and sighs of an old-style telephone when you dialed it. We are not, as our critics would claim, necessarily convinced that things were once better than they are now, nor that we ourselves, our parents, or our grandparents were happier "back then." We are simply like those savants in the Borges story who stumble upon certain objects and totems that turn out to be the random emanations and proofs of the existence of Tlön. The past is another planet; anyone ought to wonder, as we do, at any traces of it that turn up in this.

Every week, in the eight panels of a new installment of *Julius Knipl, Real Estate Photographer*, Ben Katchor manages to teleport the reader to a particular urban past—a crumbling, lunar cityscape of brick and wire that was young and raucous in the heyday of the Yellow Kid. It's a world of rumpled suits, fireproof office blocks with the date of their erection engraved on the pediment, transom windows, and harebrained if ingenious small businesses; a sleepless, hacking-cough; a dyspeptic, masculine world the color of the stained lining of a hat. (This world, in its dreamlike at times almost Dadaistic particulars, may not ever, precisely, have existed; and yet a walk through the remaining grimy, unrenovated, simulacrum-free streets of any old American downtown, with their medical-supply showrooms, flophouses, theosophical book depositories, and ninety-nine-cent stores, can be a remarkably persuasive argument for the documentary force of Katchor's work.)

But Katchor is far more than a simple archaeologist of outmoded technologies and abandoned pastimes. In fact he often plays a kind of involuted Borgesian game with the entire notion of nostalgia itself, proving that one can feel nostalgia not only for times before one's own but, surprisingly, for things that never existed. Not content or perhaps, in this age of debased nostalgia, too rigorous to evoke merely the factual elements of a vanished past so easily appropriated by admen and Republican candidates, Katchor carefully devises a seemingly endless series of regrets, in the heart of Julius Knipl, for things not only gone or rapidly disappearing, such as paper straws and television aerials, but also wholly imaginary: the Vitaloper, the Directory of the Alimentary Canal, tapeworm sanctuaries, a once-well-known brand of aerosol tranquilizer.

As, over the weeks, I joined Mr. Knipl in his peregrinations, I discovered, as will you, that the strip's wonderful evocation of an entirely plausible and heartbreaking if only partly veracious past is not the greatest of its pleasures or achievements. Ben Katchor is an extremely clever, skillful, and amusing storyteller.

With the exception of mute (and to me dreadfully tedious) strips such as *Henry* and *The Little King*, the comic strip is and has always been a literary form that braids words and pictures, inextricably, into a story. In the so-called Golden Age of the comic strip, standards with regard to both elements were often high; lately the pictures have dwindled to a bare series of thumbnail sketches, and while the notion of story has atrophied almost to nonexistence, most of the burden of humor or pathos now falls, for better or worse, on the words. But we have never—at least not since Herriman—had a writer like Katchor.

His polished, terse, and versatile prose, capable, in a single sentence strung expertly from a rhythmic frame of captions, of running from graceful elegy to police-blotter declarative to Catskill belly rumble, lays down the bare-bones elements, the newspaper-lead essentials of his story. As in all great strips, Katchor's dialogue—the hybrid element unique to comics neither quite picture nor completely words—swelling perilously inside his crooked and deformed balloons, drives, embellishes, shanghais, and comments—generally ironically—on the story, his woebegone characters sometimes echoing the taciturn elegance of the captions, sometimes speaking in an entertaining mishmash of commercial travelers' argot, Lower East Side expostulations, and the sprung accents of cheap melodrama.

None of this would mean anything, however, without Katchor's artwork, running in perpetual counterpoint to and tension with the captions and dialogue. Though his style in no way resembles that of either Jack Kirby or Will Eisner, Ben Katchor is, along with them, one of the three great depictors of New York City in the history of comics (Katchor's city, nameless or whatever its name may be, is always, plainly, New York). It is a dark, at times almost submarine city, with antecedents in sources as divergent as the work of Hopper, de Chirico, and Ditko. Wide, deserted streets find themselves hemmed in on all sides by carefully not-quite-anonymous buildings. Late-night cafeterias extrude wan panels of light onto the sidewalks. Lonely newsvendors stand beside dolmens of unsold papers.

Katchor's style, like all the great styles, is addictive. His wobbly lines, woozy perspectives, and restless shifts in point of view; his intense exploitation of a narrow spectrum of ink washes running from soot to dirty rain; his use of detail at once lavish and superbly economical, painstaking and apt; his lumbering, sad, hollow-eyed, jowly, blue-jawed men in their ill-fitting suits; his rare, mildly frightening women in their remarkable armor of trusses and lingerie—none of it is beautiful, or even, if I may be forgiven for saying so, masterly; the same could have been said about Herriman. In the funny papers a mastery of the vocabulary of comic drawing is more important than refinement of technique. Drawing skill matters only insofar as it helps the cartoonist to tell his story.

The stories Katchor tells, mostly in eight or nine panels on a single page, occasionally spilling over onto two, three, or four pages (and, wondrously, in the case of the longest and previously unpublished story in this collection, onto seventeen wild pages with an astonishing splash panel), fall, roughly, into seven categories. There are, first of all, the famous requiems for vanished places, sale items, novelties, and devices. There are episodes and accounts that serve to illuminate the ways and behaviors, from the Stasis Day Parade to the hazardous umbrella situation to the intricacies of Excursionist Drama, of the alternate Gotham in which Mr. Knipl makes his living. There are anecdotes and incidents taken from the lore of the local tradesmen, its hairstyle mappers, licensed expectorators, parked-car readers, and numerous cracked inventors. There are the odd, indirect, at times almost eventless stories so like dreams—the dreams beloved of readers of *The Evening Combinator*—that they linger and disturb. There are stories, inevitably but somehow incidentally, of Mr. Knipl himself, a lonely man in a city of lonely men, and stories of some of those other solitaires: Emmanuel Chirrup, Arthur Mammal, Carmine Delaps, Al Mooner.

In the end it isn't nostalgia but loneliness, of an impossible beauty and profundity, that is the great theme of Knipl. Katchor's city is a city of men who live alone in small apartments, tormented by memories, impracticable plans, stains on the ceiling. Small wonder, then, that they should so eagerly band together, over and over again, into the fantastic and prodigious array of clubs, brotherhoods, retirement communities, and secret societies, accounts of which make up the seventh category of Knipl story. "Fellowship," as a loyal member of the Holey Pocket league tells Mr. Knipl, "is the only thing we crave."

All seven of these typical narratives converge in *The Evening Combinator*, through whose seventeen pages Katchor begins, not without regret presumably, to effect an evacuation from the blasted country of the newspaper strip to the rumored paradise of something known, a hundred years after a bald boy in a yellow nightdress first appeared in the lonely, teeming streets of New York

City, as the graphic story. Interesting things are happening there; whether they ever reach the level of high quality combined with mass readership of the great comic strips—the creation of immense shared hallucinations—remains to be seen. Perhaps in a broken, nocturnal, past-haunted city of solitary wanderers and lunatic leagues, like this one, such universal fantasies, and the fellowship they provide, are no longer possible. No matter how we crave them. (1996)

Herma, MacDonald Harris

NO ONE OBSERVING MacDONALD HARRIS WOULD HAVE taken him for a literary genius. He did not dress head to toe in black. He never posed for a photograph in a wrestling singlet, in Zen robes, or atop a granite outcrop whose austere majesty was echoed by his windswept quiff. By September 1985, when I became his student and his friend, there was no hair at all to invite the wind's attention. The luster of his pate gave his head the appearance of the polished ball end of some precision-engineered chrome socket, or an observatory dome. You might have supposed that the mind inside that dome was busy working up new techniques of heat dissipation in airplane engines, but not new plots, new characters. He wore button-down shirts, tucked into jeans that were belted and pressed. His preferred footwear was the kind of tan hybrid of sneaker and Oxford shoe favored by elder-hostlers. Sometimes, it is true, he would wear a floppy-brimmed bucket hat and a funny kind of jacket, vaguely suggestive of an interest in trout fishing or photo safaris. But—as with the high, lustrous cranial dome—if you saw him in his goofy hat and jacket, you would have been less likely to think *There goes a literary innovator gifted with an original and unfettered artistic imagination* than *There goes a chemical engineer who enjoys cultivating succulents.*

I'm not sure whether MacDonald Harris chose to conceal himself in the guise of mild-mannered professor Donald Heiney, or if unobtrusiveness simply came as naturally to him as the making of art. I am sure—and I say this in full awareness that it takes one to know one—that the man was a freak.

I DON'T INTEND TO SUGGEST THAT HIS PSYCHOLOGY WAS IN some way aberrant or neurotic (though if his psychology was in no way aberrant or neurotic this would make him unique among writers of my acquaintance). When I say that Don was a freak, I mean to say that in his being a writer at all, as with a blue lobster or a bell-shaped tomato, there was something unaccountable and surprising. This proposition would certainly not have come as news to Don. The exceptionality of the imagination that flowered secretly in the darkness of his skull is the unstated but recurrent theme of his unpublished "Memoir of My Early Years." How the heck, Don wonders in this charming essay, considering the kind of writer he became, did that happen?

Of respectable pioneer stock, Don grew up on Oxley Street, in South Pasadena, in a seemingly placid household neither Dickensianly penurious nor Jamesianly lavish, in a family that appears to have been relatively untouched by dysfunction or defining catastrophe.

And yet, there MacDonald Harris came, fitfully, slowly, secretly into existence. The unlikelihood of this outcome, and Don's resultant view of human identity as a kind of freak accident, provides an undergirding structure of mystery to much of his work. The typical Harris novel convenes a panel of inquiry charged with explaining the beautiful accident of identity. Nowhere is this investigation conducted more thrillingly, or with greater delicacy, than in *Herma*, about a young girl who discovers that she possesses a brilliant and preposterous musical gift.

Did young Donald Heiney think of himself as a prodigy, like Herma? Not in the sense in which the word "prodigy" is commonly employed. The "Memoir" describes an early infatuation with reading that worried his parents. It struck them as uncanny, unnerving, the way Herma's singing unnerves her parents. And it's in this sense that Don's reconfiguring of his childhood as the childhood of a prodigy ought to be understood.

The etymological roots of the word "prodigy"—like those of "monster"—lie in the uncanny, in the unaccountable appearance of portents: an eclipse, the birth of a goat with two heads. A prodigy makes manifest the cryptic nature of the gods' intentions. It reveals the fundamental truth of the universe: that the fundamental truth of the universe will remain forever concealed.

It is a proven tendency of families to view an incipient writer in their midst as a kind of monster. Whether they have the blessing or disapproval of their families, writers grow up feeling that they do not belong in the house they were born into. Writers are mutants; some crucial part of their existential DNA is unshared with their parents or siblings.

I remember a conversation I had with Don, in which it emerged that we were both ardent admirers of Borges's short story "The House of Asterion," a retelling of the myth of the Minotaur from the monster's lonely point of view.

Don said that it was Borges's genius to see the minotaur as a prince, as part of a family, the son of King Minos and Queen

Pasiphaë, the brother of Princess Ariadne. For the family of a writer, as for the Royal Family of Crete, there will be always a monster in the house: a creature who remembers things nobody else seems to remember, notices things everyone else seems to have missed, wonders things that no one else would ever bother to wonder; a creature who comes to dwell at the heart of a labyrinth of his or her own making—a labyrinth of words.

No doubt much could be written about the genitally expressed nature of Herma's particular form of freakishness (quite apart from her singing ability), and what that strange sexual convertibility might or might not reveal about the proclivities of her (and eventually his) creator. Suffice to say that the longing for some kind of crystalline inner unity runs all the way through MacDonald Harris's work, and he found many other ways of expressing that longing besides this book about a girl named Herma who can turn herself, at will and thanks to the remarkable agility of certain of her nether muscles, into a boy named Fred.

You don't have to be a sexual dimorph, or a writer, to believe that a crucial part of yourself remains forever hidden, that you will never feel whole. That, finally, is what makes *Herma* important to me. With all the vigor, perfection of sentence, and obsessiveness of research that make all his books so rewarding, MacDonald Harris—aka Donald Heiney, the secret minotaur of Oxley Street— managed to capture, as no other writer ever quite has, the isolation and the yearning that make freaks not just of minotaurs, writers, and hermaphrodites, but of us all. (2015)

Casting the Runes and Other Ghost Stories, M. R. James

I'LL JUST COME RIGHT OUT AND SAY IT. I THINK THAT M. R. James's "Oh, Whistle, and I'll Come to You, My Lad" is one of the finest short stories ever written. The problematic term in that last sentence, of course, is not "finest" but "short stories." It's a mark of how radically we have changed our ideas of what a short story, and in particular a fine one, ought to be, that there should be something odd about ranking this masterpiece of the Other James in the same league with, say, "The Real Thing" or "Four Meetings." The ghost story has been consigned to the ghetto of subgenre. Rare is the contemporary anthology of "best short stories of all time" that includes even a token example of the form.

Once it was not thus. Once, you could argue, the ghost story *was* the genre itself. Balzac, Poe, de Maupassant, Kipling—most of the early inventors—wrote ghost stories as a matter of course, viewing them as a fundamental of the storyteller's craft. Edith Wharton was an enthusiast and master of the "subgenre"; I think her ghost stories are the cream of her short fiction. And Henry James himself, of course, gave us the one ghost story whose status as literature is not open to debate: "The Turn of the Screw." It was only the best of a good two dozen that he produced during the heyday of the form, in the latter half of the nineteenth century.

Maybe our taste has grown more refined, or our understanding of human psychology more subtle. Maybe we don't really believe in ghosts anymore. Or maybe for the past sixty years or so we've simply been cheating ourselves, we lovers of the short story, out of one of the genre's enduring pleasures.

A great ghost story is *all* psychology: in careful and accurate detail it presents (1) a state of perception, by no means rare in human experience, in which the impossible vies with the undeniable evidence of the senses; and (2) the range of emotions brought on by that perception. And then, by the quantum strangeness of literature, it somehow manages to engender these same emotions in the reader: the prickling nape, the racing heart, the sense of some person standing invisibly near. Everyone has felt such things, coming up the basement stairs with darkness at our backs, turning around at the sound of a footstep to find only an empty room. I once saw a face, intelligent and smiling, formed from the dappled shadow of a stucco ceiling in a Los Angeles bedroom. The face remained, perfectly visible to both my wife and me, until we finally turned out the light. The next morning it was gone. Afterward, no matter how we looked at the ceiling, in daylight or at night, the face failed to reappear. I have never to this day forgotten its mocking leer as it studied me.

It is tempting to say that, like his contemporaries Algernon Blackwood and Arthur Machen, Montague Rhodes James is something of a ghost himself, nowadays, at least in the United States. He haunts the pages of dusty anthologies with titles like *Classic Chilling Stories of Terror and Suspense*, his name lapsed into obscurity along with those of the authors of durable gems of the genre such as "The Beckoning Fair One" (Oliver Onions) and "The Monkey's Paw" (W. W. Jacobs). But in England he is still remembered, and even beloved. James is about as English as it is possible for an English writer to be. A hungry anglophile, one with no interest whatever (if such a creature exists) in the ghosts that haunt old abbeys, dusty libraries, and the Saxon churches of leafy villages, could survive very happily on a steady diet of M. R. James. These are stories that venture to the limits of the human capacity for terror and revulsion, as it were, armed only with an umbrella and a very dry wit. They are still read aloud on the radio over there, in particular at Christmastime when, as during the season that frames "The Turn of the Screw," it is apparently traditional to sit by a crackling Yule fire and scare one's friends out of their wits. (And it would be hard to imagine anything more English than that.)

M. R. James presents a nearly unique instance in the history of supernatural literature—perhaps in the history of literature, period: he seems, for the entire duration of his life (1865–1936) to have considered himself the happiest of men. His biography, insofar as it has been written, is free of the usual writerly string of calamities and reversals, of intemperate behavior, self-destructive partnerings, critical lambasting, poverty, illness, and bad luck. His childhood, though it sounds to modern ears to have been a tad heavy on devotional exercise, Christian study, and mindfulness of the sufferings of Jesus and his saints, was passed in material comfort and within the loving regard of his parents and older siblings; the candle-lit gloom of the paternal church counterbalanced, if balance were needed, by ready access to the beauties of the East Anglian countryside that surrounded his father's rectory. His early school years were notable, if at all, only for the consistent excellence of his academic performance and for the popularity he attained among his fellow students, in part through a discovered knack for spinning a first-class frightening tale. At the age of fourteen he entered the world of Eton and, though he spent the middle portion of his life as a laureate, Fellow, and finally Dean of King's College, Cambridge (itself a sister school to Eton), he never really left that sheltered, companionable green and gray world, assuming at last the mantle of Provost of Eton in 1918, a position he held until he died. He was a brilliant, prize-winning, internationally known scholar of early Christian manuscripts who devoted his personal life to enlarging, slowly and knowledgeably, his circle of gentleman friends, a task made simpler by his brilliance, charm, wit, kindness, and affability. He took no interest in politics, involved his name in no controversy or cause, and traveled in comfort through Denmark, Sweden, France, and other of the tamer corners of the globe. The seeker after shadows who turns, in desperation, to discover what untold sufferings James, like H. C. Anderson or E. A. Poe, might have undergone for the love of a woman, will discover here a profound silence. James never married, and as far as we are allowed to determine, the complete absence of romantic attachments in his life caused him no pain or regret whatsoever.

And the childhood fascination with the tortures suffered by Christian martyrs, each date and gruesome detail of beheadings, immolations, and dismemberments lovingly memorized the way some boys memorize batting averages? And the spectral face at the garden gate, pale and wild-eyed and reeking of evil that one evening peered back at the young James across the lawn as he looked out through the windows of the rectory? And the intimate eleven-year friendship with a man named McBryde, illustrator of some of James's best stories, traveling companion and inseparable confidant, whose rather late marriage, in 1903, was followed, scarcely a year later, by his untimely death? And the boys, the tens upon hun-

dreds upon thousands of boys of Eton and King's, on whom James
had lavished his great teacherly gifts, cut down in the battlefields
of Belgium and France? And the empty lawns, deserted commons
and dining halls, the utter desolation of Cambridge in 1918?

Over all of this speculation as to the origins of James's ghosts
and horrors, over any hint of torment, shame, passion, remorse, or
sorrow, the shutters have been drawn. The only evidence we have
for the existence of such emotions in M. R. James is the disturbing
tales he chose, over and over, to tell. Could they possibly be the
work of a man whose life presented him with a nearly unbroken
series of comfortable, satisfying, and gratifying days, from cradle
to grave? Let us say that they could; let us stipulate that the stories
are the work of a man whom life denied none of the fundamentals
of mortal happiness. Violence, horror, grim retribution, the sudden
revulsion of the soul—these things, then, are independent of happiness or suffering; a man who looks closely and carefully at life,
whether pitiable as Poe or enviable as the Provost of Eton, cannot
fail to see them.

Along with A. E. Housman, Thomas Hardy, and even, we are
told, Theodore Roosevelt, one of James's early admirers was the
American horror writer H. P. Lovecraft (1890–1937). The two
men shared a taste for old books and arcane manuscripts, for dusty
museums and the libraries of obscure historical societies, and for
ancient buildings, in particular those equipped with attics and
crypts; shared that requisite of any great writer of ghost stories: a
hyperacute sense of the past. We all have this sixth human sense, to
one degree or another, but in the case of Lovecraft and James the
sense of the past is as evolved as the sense of smell in a professional
nez. When it comes to their writing, however, Lovecraft and James
could not differ more—in style, in scale, in temperament. Lovecraft's style is the despair of the lover of Lovecraft, at once shrill

and vague, clotted, pedantic, hysterical, and sometimes out-and-out bad. James, on the other hand, writes the elegant English sentences, agile and reticent, that an excellent British education of his era both demanded and assured. The contrast is particularly stark when it comes to their portrayal of the un-portrayable. Lovecraft approaches Horror armed with adverbs, abstractions, and perhaps a too-heavy reliance on pseudopods and tentacles. James rarely does more than hint at the nature of his ghosts and apparitions, employing a few simple, select, revolting adjectives, summoning his ghosts into hideous, enduring life in the reader's mind in a bare sentence or two.

Evil, in Lovecraft, is universal, pervasive, and at least partially explicable in terms of notions such as Elder Races and blind idiot gods slobbering at the heart of creation. In James, Evil tends to have more of a local feel, somehow, assembling itself at times out of the most homely materials; and yet to remain, in the end, beyond any human explanation whatsoever. Evil is strangely rationalized in Lovecraft, irresistible but systematic; it can be sought, and found. In James it irrupts, is chanced upon, brushes against our lives, irrevocably, often when we are looking in the other direction. But the chief difference between Lovecraft and James was one of temperament. Lovecraft, apart from a few spasmodic periods, including one in which he briefly married a Brooklyn Jew named Sonia Greene and formed a part of her salon—liked his own company best. He could be gloomy and testy, and was perhaps most appreciated by his friends at a distance, through his lively correspondence with them. M. R. James, on the other hand, was legendary for his conviviality, and loved nothing more than whiling away an afternoon in sherry and tobacco with his erudite friends. Indeed, friends—colleagues, companions—play an important role in James's stories, coming along to shore up the protagonist's courage at just the right moment, providing him with moral support, crucial information, or simply another soul with whom to share an unspeakable secret. In Lovecraft the protagonist has often cut himself off from his friends and companions, and must face the final moment of slithering truth alone.

Lovecraft wrote, in part, for money, often as little as one and a half cents a word; James was an avowed hobbyist of literature, and wrote many of his finest stories as Christmas entertainments of the sort already described, reading them aloud to his assembled friends by the light of a single candle. These lucky men were every bit as entertained by them as you will be. The stories are, nevertheless, unmistakably works of art, the products of a peculiar imagination, a moral sense at once keen and undogmatic, and an artist's scientific eye for shape and structure.

This brings us back to "Oh, Whistle, and I'll Come to You, My Lad," whose unlucky protagonist, Parkes, we first encounter in conversation with his fellow professors over dinner "in the hospitable hall of St. James's college." (James's stories never originate in cheap atmospherics, fogs or plagues or blasted landscapes, or with the creaky, dubious avowals of narratorial sanity so beloved of Lovecraft and Poe.) In the very first sentence James displays the remarkable command that qualifies him as a great unrecognized master of point of view, which is the ultimate subject of any ghost story and, of course, of twentieth-century literature itself. For the narrator, or the author, or some indeterminate, playful amalgam of the two, reveals himself before we are twenty words into the story, and will continue to remind us of his presence throughout, right up to the final paragraph when at last he takes leave, with a strange kind of cheerful pity, of the shattered Professor Parkes.

I don't think any writer has handled a narrator in quite the same way as James in "Oh, Whistle." For the narrator here is not merely a disembodied authorial voice in the classic nineteenth-century manner. He is *involved* in the lives of the characters he describes, he *knows* them, he sees them on a regular basis—he is, albeit invisibly, a character in the story, cut from the same cloth, as it were, as Parkes and Rogers and the rest of the St. James's faculty. There are portions of the story, he suggests, that *could* be told, that actually happened—most of them having to do with the game of golf—but which he gratefully lacks the expertise to set down. This accords with a fundamental operation of the supernatural story, from "The Facts in the Case of M. Valdemar" to "The Blair Witch Project," which is to make the explicit point—generally implicit or finessed in "literary" fiction—that what is being given is *a factual account*. All ghost stories are "true" stories. We love them, if we love them, from the depth and antiquity of our willingness to believe them.

M. R. James, more than any other writer, explores the wobble, the shimmer of uncertainty that results when quotation marks are placed around the word "true." Because at the same time that the narrator of "Oh, Whistle" is implicating himself in his story—scrupulously telling us what he has seen for himself and what parts of the story he has only heard second- or thirdhand—his supremely "authoritative" voice and evident easy control over the materials establish him as unmistakably the *writer* of the story, its inventor, hurrying us past characters we need not overly attend to, rendering the events with an impossible familiarity. This, in turn, calls into question the fictional status of the narrator, and hence that of the author himself.

All of this, I know, sounds dreadfully postmodern. And indeed James, not merely in his approach, at once careful and cavalier, to point of view, but also in fitting out his stories with the full apparatus of scholarly research—footnotes, learned quotations from Latin, references to obscure medieval tracts—often anticipates

Borges and the postmodernists, and with every iota of their self-conscious playfulness. But the playfulness is worn so lightly, and the experiments in point of view are undertaken with such a practical purpose—scaring you—in mind, that even a critical reader may scarcely be aware of them the first time through. James is like some casual, gentleman tinkerer yoking a homemade anti-gravity drive to the derailleurs of his bicycle because he is tired of being late to church every Sunday.

"Oh, Whistle, and I'll Come to You, My Lad" is, in many ways, the prototypical M. R. James story. It presents a man who stumbles, through generally benevolent motives (Parkes, in searching the Templar ruin that conceals the fatal flute, is mostly trying to help his archaeologist colleague, and to give the outraged Colonel a chance to cool down), upon a historical puzzle that cannot fail to interest him and, poking innocently around in it, inadvertently summons—more literally here than in other stories—an unexpected revenant of a bygone time, with frightful results.

The story is typical of James, as well, in that when at last we encounter the Horror, there is something about its manifestation, its physical attributes, its *habits*, that puts the reader in mind, however reluctantly, of sex. I say reluctantly in part because the cool, fleshy, pink, protruberant, furred, toothed or mouthed apparations one finds in M. R. James are so loathsome; and in part because James keeps his stories studiously free—swept clean—not merely of references to sexual behavior but of all the hot-and-heavy metaphor and overt Freudian paraphernalia with which supernatural fiction is so often encumbered. James is a hospitable writer, and one wishes not to offend one's host. But the fact remains that "Oh, Whistle, and I'll Come to You, My Lad" is a story about a man pursued into the darkness of a strange bedroom, and all of the terror is ultimately generated by a vision of a horribly disordered bed. The bodily horror, the uncanny, even repulsive nature of sex—a favorite theme of the genre from Stoker to Cronenberg—is a recurring element in the stories of M. R. James, rendered all the more potent because it feels so genuinely *unconscious*. Sex was undoubtedly the last thing on the mind of M. R. James as he sat down to compose his Christmas creepers, but it is often the first Thing to emerge when the stays of reality are loosened.

At times, as in traditional ghost stories (e.g., "A Christmas Carol"), James's characters engender and deserve their ghastly fates, bringing them about through excess of ambition, pride, or greed. Professor Parkes, one senses, does not entirely meet with the author's approval—he is priggish, skeptical; he plays golf—but in other stories the protagonists are men whose profession, temperament, and tastes barely distinguish them from their creator. Most of the time they are innocents, ignorant trippers and travelers who brush up against the omnipresent meaningless malevolence of the world, and the sins for which they are punished tend, likely as not, to be virtues—curiosity, honesty, a sympathy for bygone eras, a desire to do honor to one's ancestors. And, often, their punishment is far grimmer than the scare that Professor Parkes receives.

The secret power of James's work lies in his steadfast refusal fully to explain, in the end, the mechanisms that have brought about the local irruption of Evil he describes, and yet to leave us, time and again, utterly convinced that such an explanation is possible, if only we were in possession of all facts. He makes us *feel* the logic of haunting, the residue of some inscrutable chain of ghostly causation, though we can't—though, he insists, we *never will be able to*—explain or understand that logic. In "Oh, Whistle," the elements—the Templars' church, the brass flute with its fragmentary inscriptions, the blind pursuing figure in white, the whistled-up wind—all hang together seamlessly in the reader's imagination: they fit. And yet, in the end, we have no idea why. For the central story of M. R. James, reiterated with inexhaustible inventiveness, is ultimately the breathtaking fragility of life, of "reality," of all the structures that we have erected to defend ourselves from our constant nagging suspicion that underlying everything is chaos, brutal and unreasoning. It is hard to conceive of a more serious theme, or a more contemporary plot, than this.

It may be, in fact, that the ghost story, like the dinosaur, is still very much with us, transformed past the point of ready recognition into the feathered thing that we call "the modern short story." All short stories, in other words, are ghost stories, accounts of visitations and reckonings with the traces of the past. They describe moments when a dark door, long closed, is opened, when a forgotten error is unwittingly repeated, when the fabric of a life is revealed to have been woven, from frail and dubious fiber, over top of something unknowable and possibly very bad. Were there ever characters in fiction more haunted than Chekhov's or Joyce's by ghosts? (2002)

Brown Sugar Kitchen, Tanya Holland

OAKLAND—LIKE A SWINGING PARTY, LIKE AN EMERGENCY— is happening. Oakland is *always* happening. From the moment of its founding, in the 1850s, by a nefarious confederation of squatters, opportunists, filibusterers, graft artists, boosters, visionary thieves, and confidence men, Bump City has been happening. And yet, in all that time, Oakland has never quite *happened*. Or rather, Oakland never *has happened*. Oakland has never had its day. It has never gone soft, grown fat, rested on its laurels. It has never entirely gotten its act together, remembered to set its alarm clock, made it through to payday, waited for its cake to cool completely. There *is* a there there (Oakland coolly says "Bite me" to Gertrude Stein), but Oakland's not there yet.

Getting there, though. Oakland is—always, forever—getting there.

Oakland is like America in that way. Oakland's like America in a lot of ways—violent and peace-loving, burdened by a calamitous racial history, factious and muddled, friendly and casual, rich in local genius and in natural beauty, poorly governed, sweet-natured, cold-eyed, out to lunch, out for blood, out for a good time. And, above all, *promising*. Every day, Oakland makes and breaks the American promise, a promise so central to the idea of America that we carry it around everywhere we go, in our wallets, jingling in our pockets. I mean, of course, *e pluribus unum*: out of all the scattered sparks, one shining light. It's a utopian promise, and like all utopian promises, liable to breakage. But even if that promise can never truly be redeemed, it can be—it must be—endlessly *renewed*. And it's the work that we put in, day after day, toward renewing the promise, and not the promise's fulfillment, that really matters.

Tanya Holland knows that. Every day, starting at 5:30 a.m., she renews Oakland's promise at Brown Sugar Kitchen, a little hip-pocket utopia in the city's wild west end. Of all the many good restaurants, greasy-spoon to top-drawer, that make up a substantial share of the cultural wealth of Oakland, Tanya's Brown Sugar Kitchen most clearly, most faithfully, and most thrillingly embodies, one plate of chicken and waffles at a time, the ongoing, ever-renewed promise of the city she has come to love and, in a very real sense, to embody.

Drop by Brown Sugar Kitchen any day, for breakfast or lunch, and you will find people of all ages and stations, professing various brands of faith or doubt, tracing their ancestries to Africa and Europe, Asia and South America, to the Cherokee, Shawnee, or Creek. You might very well find all those inheritances gathered around a single table, perhaps even in the genetic code of a single member of the waitstaff.

Diversity in the kitchen and dining room is hardly unusual in an Oakland restaurant, of course—that's one of the things to love about Oakland. Even in cities segregated far more determinedly than Oakland, I've noticed that a popular soul-food restaurant will often feature the most integrated tables in town—that's one of the things to love about soul food. Beans, rice, and collards are a powerful force for transformation. But the crowd's different at Brown Sugar Kitchen. More jumbled, the lines of race and class drawn more faintly than in Oakland's other restaurants, soul food or otherwise. A more purposive clientele, I want to say, *self*-jumbled, everybody showing up with his or her own eraser to rub away those lines a little more. One of the most beautiful things about human beings, in the midst of so much that is ugly, is the desire that takes hold of us, if only we can manage to leave our homes, our villages, and our little worlds behind, for the companionship of people from Elsewhere. Make no mistake; people come to Brown Sugar Kitchen for the food. I believe that I could be hauled back from the gates of the Underworld by the prospect of a bowl of Tanya's shrimp and grits. But it was Oakland, and not some other town, remember, that cradled the visions of the most high prophet Sly Stone, and to a greater extent than I've found in other American cities, the Everyday People of Oakland are hip to the possibility that the point of the journey is neither the destination *nor* the journey itself but rather the coming to a crossroads, to a watering hole, to what my character Archy Stallings, in *Telegraph Avenue,* likes to call a "caravansary." The point of the journey, to the everyday wanderer, is the feeling one gets on crossing the threshold of one of those magical places along the way, built on the borderline between here and there, where the stories and the homelands and the crooked routes of history come together in a slice of sweet potato pie.

Maybe the word I'm looking for to describe the spirit that imbues the patrons and the principals of Brown Sugar Kitchen is something more like "mindfulness." (An East Bay word if there ever was one.) As lovers of Oakland, Tanya and her husband, Phil Surkis, are *mindful* that the neighborhood where they chose to build their caravansary is the broken heart of Oakland, the place where all those industrious scoundrels who afterward lent their names to streets and civic buildings first conspired to defraud the Peralta family of their land. All the paths of ancestry and migration taken by Oakland's founding peoples—Indian, Spanish, Mexican, Anglo-, Asian-, and African-American—are densely knotted in West Oakland, with its physical routes and roadways, its boulevards and streets. West Oakland is the great crossroads of the city's history, the stage and the scene of its starkest crimes and dramas, its most tragic comedies, from the founding land grab to the glory of the Pullman strikes, from the apocalyptic destruction rained down by Federal urban policy in the sixties to the collapse of the Great Beast of Urban Renewal, the Cypress Freeway, during the Loma Prieta earthquake of 1989. The Black Panthers, the Oakland Oaks, shipbuilders and railway workers, immigrant Jews and Portuguese, Okies and followers of the Great Migration, all came and went along Market and Cypress and West Street, as neighborhoods rose and fell, and Huey P. Newton got murdered, and the industrial demands of two world wars brought a measure of security and comfort, often for the first time, to people whose status had been marginal and precarious. Tanya and Phil were mindful, in choosing the site for their caravansary, that there could be no better place than along the Mandela Parkway, the enchanted road that grew up, gracious and wide and landscaped with greenery, in the gap that had once been the dark underbelly of the Cypress Freeway.

Tanya showed the same mindfulness in conceiving her Kitchen, in formulating her recipes, in committing herself to the cooking of soul food. This was, by her own admission, an unexpected choice. She had come west with plans to open a place that would showcase her La Varenne training; but then she dialed in to the local vibe, to the Sly Stone vision, to that Oakland state of mind.

And one day she found herself standing on the 2500 block of the Mandela Parkway, feeling those paths of ancestry, those trails and roads and streets and railheads all coming together in the great soul terminus of West Oakland, and determined to set up shop, there, along the banks of the Mandela, and lay down her own artful and inspired version of the Oakland promise in the form of po' boys, roux, and waffles.

Consciously or intuitively—mindfully—Tanya made this culinary choice, I believe, because the cuisine we know as soul food—so styled sometime in the 1950s, around the time rhythm and blues was becoming *soul music*—comes closer than any other product of American art and ingenuity to redeeming the promise of *e pluribus unum*. Peanuts, rice, okra, and yams from Africa; Central American beans and cassava; European pork, cabbage, molasses, and turnips; Indian corn and hominy, berries and greens: soul food is the caravansary along the road from the African past to the American present, from freedom to slavery to freedom again. Soul food is the little joint at the broken heart of America where all the kitchen inheritances ingather, and get tangled like travelers' yarns, like the paths of exile and homecoming, like strands of DNA. From the day she opened her little utopia on the Mandela Parkway, Tanya has been making and keeping and redeeming her promise: Come on in, all of you everyday wanderers, and take a seat, and I will feed your soul. Oh—and come hungry. (2014)

Monster Man, Gary Gianni

W<small>E WHO HAVE CREWED ABOARD</small> C<small>APTAIN</small> N<small>EMO'S</small> *N<small>AUTILUS</small>* have been left by the experience—in all its antique and tempestuous splendor—with a certain look. We recognize one another, even across great distances and gulfs of years. I remember first encountering the work of my fellow Nautilusard Gary Gianni in the illustrations he did for the marvelous Wandering Star editions of the works of Robert E. Howard. I knew him at once: a sailor of the deeps of popular art and literature; a mapper of submerged, half-forgotten kingdoms with names like Valusia and Atlantis and the Misty Isles. And yet never—or never merely—a diver to the benthos and bathos of nostalgia. Our ship, remember, is state of the art, at once the premier and dernier cri of the modernity that Jules Verne arguably invented. The first gesture of modernity is to explode the past and sweep away its fragments. The second is to use those very fragments to construct new art in the landscape and language of brokenness. I saw in Gianni's classic pen-and-ink style, in the panache of his cross-hatching, in his mastery of black, in the dynamic flow of his composition and figures, in the evident breadth of Gianni's familiarity with the history of adventure illustration, a third gesture: the modernity of the *Nautilus*. We do not seek to rise to the surface of history like a sleeper surfacing from a nightmare. We do not dangle our little lines from cobbled boats, fishing up the bits and pieces. The sea is our home. We swim through it, in the state-of-the-art, electric-powered submarine of our imaginations, drawing freely upon it for everything we need. We are practical modernists. Where others become entangled in vast kelp beds of history, we roll cigars. I was not at all surprised to discover, shortly after that first encounter with Gianni, that he had (studiously, gloriously, and with his customary élan) adapted *20,000 Leagues Under the Sea* as a graphic novel.

If that book, and some of the other work that Gary Gianni has done in comics, like the weekly *Prince Valiant* page, exhibits a certain stateliness, an air of pageantry—if it never quite abandoned the illustrative tradition of which Gianni is a master—*Monsterman* leaves no doubt: the dude knows how to rock a comic book page. In addition to all his usual swash and shadow, the easy grace of his figures, the depth and dynamism of his layouts, in these pages you will find Gianni putting on a clinic in the art of page layout, showing the degree to which he has pragmatically absorbed the lessons of layout saboteurs like Eisner and Chaykin and Miller—the Captain Nemos, romantic destroyers of the comics page—and married them to the Gianni style, nourished and enriched by the past as the crew of Nautilus by the bounty of the deep. Add to this a reinvention of the figure of the Occult Detective, steeped like everything Gianni does in a grasp of its history from Carnacki to Hellboy, and the result is thrilling, almost disturbing, and it brings us, out of the sea-bottom of the past, as all art must, something new. (2012)

The Sailor on the Seas of Fate, Michael Moorcock

THE *SAILOR ON THE SEAS OF FATE,* LIKE ALMOST ALL OF MICHAEL Moorcock's efforts in the subgenre of heroic fantasy, is a complicated work, in the original sense of the term: that is, it *folds together*, with an insight both sophisticated and intuitive, (1) an apparently simple adventure story told in three episodes that are themselves interleaved in puzzling ways; (2) a sharp critique of adventure stories generally (with their traditional freight of cruelty, wish-fulfillment, sexism, and violence) and of the heroic fantasy mode in particular; and (3) a remarkable working out (independently one feels of the work of Joseph Campbell) of the Transcendentalist premise that, as Emerson wrote, "one person wrote all the books." Moorcock took this literary universalism, with its implied corollary that one person *reads* all the books, and in *Sailor* began his career-long demonstration of the logical conclusion that all the books are one book, and all the heroes one hero (or antihero). From here it is only a short step, which the reader of heroic fantasy is eager to make, to the proposition that all readers and all writers are Odysseus, or Kull, or Elric of Melniboné, sharing through the acts of reading and writing a single essential, eternal heroic nature. This nature links us—all we heroes and Moorcocks—across all eras and lands. One might even attempt to chart these interconnections of story, hero, reader, and writer on a single map: Moorcock is such a cartographer. He called his map of our story-shaped world "the Multiverse."

It was Moorcock's insight, and it has been his remarkable artistic accomplishment, not just to complicate all this apparatus and insight and storytelling prowess, packing into one short novel such diverting fare as speculation on ontology and determinism, gory subterranean duels with giant killer baboons, literary criticism (the murmuring soul-vampiric sword Stormbringer offers what is essentially a running commentary on the equivocal nature of heroic swordsmen in fiction), buildings that are really alien beings, and ruminations on the self-similar or endlessly reflective interrelationship of hero, writer, and reader; but to do so with an almost offhanded ease, with a strong, plain, and unaffected English prose style that was nearing its peak in the mid-seventies.

That's part of what I would have liked to tell to Michael Moorcock when I recently had the good fortune to attend the Nebula Awards ceremony in Austin, Texas, and watch him receive a Grandmaster Award. I would have liked to tell him that when I was fourteen years old I found profound comfort in feeling that I shared in the nature of lost and wandering Elric, isolated but hungering for connection, heroically curious, apparently weak but capable of surprising power, unready and unwilling to sit on the moldering throne of his fathers but having nothing certain to offer in its stead. I would have liked to tell him that his work as a critic, as an editor, and as a writer has made it easier for me and a whole generation of us to roam the "moonbeam roads" of the literary multiverse. But as Mike rose to accept his award all I could do was sit there, next to him—marveling down to the deepest most twisted strands of my literary DNA—and applaud. (2013)

American Flagg!, Howard Chaykin

I.

In a popular medium that needs to label everyone a journeyman hack or a flaming genius god—like the world of comic book art—Howard Chaykin is something else: a craftsman, an artisan of pop.

I don't mean that Chaykin works harder on or takes greater pains with his drawing, though his panels and his layouts bear witness to the pains he takes (like many craftsmen he actually works rather fast). Nor do I mean merely that he brings deeper technical prowess to the comics page (though when it comes to page design, panel arrangement, line control, and the rendering of bodies, faces, clothing, streets, furniture, and interiors, his chops are matchless). Some of the genius gods of comic art, after all, have also been master draftsmen; and one of the best things about popular media is that, within their capital- and calendar-driven confines, sometimes a hack, half by accident, can turn out something haunting, dreamy, or beautiful. What I'm talking about is a kind—the toughest kind—of balancing act. Taking pains, working hard, not flaunting his or her chops so much as relying on them, the pop artisan teeters on a fine fulcrum between the stern, sell-the-product morality of the workhorse and the artist's urge to discover a pattern in, or derive a meaning from, the random facts of the world. Like those other postwar, East Coast Jewish boys, Barry Levinson and Paul Simon, Chaykin, a man as gifted with a quicksilver intelligence, an irrepressible sense of verbal play, and reservoirs of rage and humor of apparently equal depth, has spent most of his career seeking, and sometimes finding, that difficult equilibrium.

The pop artisan operates within the received formulas—gangster movie, radio-ready A-side, space opera—and then incorporates into the style, manner, and mood of the work bits and pieces derived from all the aesthetic moments he or she has ever fallen in love with, in other movies or songs or novels, whether hackwork or genius (without regard for and sometimes without consciousness of any difference between the two): the bridge in a song by the Moonglows, a James Wong Howe camera angle, a Sabatini cannonade, a Stan Getz solo, the climax of *The Demolished Man*, a locomotive design by Raymond Loewy, a Shecky Green routine. When it works, what you get is not a collection of references, quotes, allusions, and cribs but a whole, seamless thing, both familiar and new: a record of the consciousness that was busy falling in love with those moments in the first place. It's that filtering consciousness, coupled with the physical ability (or whatever it is) to flat-out play or sing or write or draw, that transforms the fragments and jetsam and familiar pieces into something fresh and unheard of. If that sounds a lot like what flaming genius gods are supposed to be up to, then here's a distinction: the pop artisan is always hoping that, in the end, the thing is going to be Huge. He is haunted by a vision of pop perfection: heartbreaking beauty that moves units. The closest that Howard Chaykin has yet come to fulfilling that vision—though he has approached it many times—is probably still *American Flagg!*

2.

BY 1982, THE WELL-ESTABLISHED SF TROPE OF A DYSTOPIAN FU-ture America (or of a solar or galactic federation closely extrapolated from the American model), dominated by giant conglomerates, plastered with video screens and advertisements, awash in fe-tishized sex and sexualized commodities, fed and controlled and defined by pharmacology and violence, had been working its way into mainstream comic books for several years, particularly at Marvel. Just as Golden Age comic books had been influenced (and in some cases written) by the hacks and flaming geniuses of the slightly earlier Golden Age of science fiction, many of the creators of early- to mid-seventies comic books showed the influence of sf's New Wave of the previous decade. The psychotic megalo-cities and paranoid technoscapes pioneered in 1940s sf by Alfred Bester (far ahead of his time and sadly neglected today), and further ex-plored by Phillip K. Dick, William S. Burroughs, Harlan Ellison, J. G. Ballard, Michael Moorcock, and John Brunner, were reflected in titles like Rich Buckler's *Deathlok the Demolisher*, Jim Starlin's *War-lock*, and the work, across many genres and titles, of Steve Gerber. Little by little, comics, along with the rest of us, began to surrender the old World's Fair–cum–Jetsons vision of the way things were going to be.

3.

BY THE TIME CHAYKIN BROUGHT OUT *American Flagg!*, IN 1982, therefore, the idea of a science fiction comic book set in a dystopian American future was not a new one; and most of the fundamental elements of the world Chaykin depicts—Earth abandoned by its corporate rulers in favor of off-world colonies, marauding gangs of armed motorcycle freaks, the city as a kind of vast television or information screen that irradiates or medicates its denizens with psychotropic sitcoms—could be traced back to novels by the writers of the New Wave and their successors, to *Rollerball* and, of course, to *Blade Runner* (1982, directed by Ridley Scott, another pop artisan, and itself based on a Dick novel), which premiered about a year before *American Flagg!* But no one had ever before crammed those elements all together in quite the way that Chaykin did here: the post-nuclear, post-global-collapse, post–Cold War, corporate-controlled, media-overloaded, sex-driven, space-traveling, Jean-Paul-Gaultier-by-way-of-Albert-Speer freak-o-rama that was to be life in 2031.

What Chaykin uniquely intuited, perhaps through the process of adapting Bester in the early graphic novel *The Stars My Destination* (New York: Baronet, 1979), was that with its fundamental liability to fragmentation, juxtaposition, and the layering up of text and images; with its multiple margins into which ever denser images and subtexts and submargins could be crammed; with its ability to hyper-jump a million light-years out to the edge of the galaxy in the space of a quarter-inch gap between panels; with its mongrel vocabulary, its clandestine heritage of sex and violence, its nature as corporate-owned media outlet and mass-produced object; and above all with its accumulated history of stale, outmoded, and rotting bright futures, the comic book was perfectly suited not

merely to adapting but in some measure to embodying the hybrid-
ized, trashy, garish future of simulacra and ad copy that comics
had been hinting at over the past decade. Other comic creators
had written or drawn the American dystopia; Howard Chaykin
went and built one.

4.

I FEAR I HAVE MADE THE PROSPECT OF READING *AMERICAN FLAGG!*
sound like a grim, possibly even a dreadful task. In fact, from the first
panel the strip, almost twenty-five years later, remains completely
exhilarating. Part of the reason for this is the virtuoso display Chaykin puts on, with a certain vandalistic Brooklyn-boy glee, of how
utterly to scramble the standard deck of page layouts that comic
book artists had been shuffling and reshuffling for years. Chaykin
played, dazzlingly, with the effect you could get from just a handful
of dull square subpanels arranged across a big single-panel page on
which, in that one big panel, something violent and wild was taking
place. All that gorgeous Caniffian line, putting the flutter into a lacy
cuff, setting a gleam on the visor of a leather hat, flinging a spray
of blood into the air, all that lavish nonchalant beauty plastered
over with Jewish gags, neon signs, talking-head nattering, tough-
guy commentary, scientific annotation! If Chaykin's work comes
squarely out of the tradition of comics art that likes to stand back
and notice how pretty it is—a tradition that includes such greats as
Alex Raymond, Mac Raboy, Jim Steranko, Barry Windsor-Smith,
and Neal Adams—it is perhaps unique in that it also derives, less
obviously, from another grand comics tradition from E. Segar to
Al Capp to Kurtzman and the *Mad* men to Kyle Baker: the tradition of mocking word-play, snide commentary, caricature, and the

irrepressible, compulsive, sometimes perilous need to undercut more or less everything but especially comics art that likes to stand back and notice how pretty it is.

The characteristic Chaykin facial expression is the raised eyebrow—of irony, skepticism, puckishness, a satirist's rage. In his work, on his characters' faces, the raised eyebrow takes on an iconic power. It's a combination of punctuation mark, the line that indicates a flexing muscle, and the kind of ripple or wave that cartoonists use to suggest motion, explosion, velocity, shock. I have never seen a published photo of Chaykin in which he fails to sport one himself.

5.

PEOPLE HAVE BEEN IMITATING, SWIPING FROM, AND BUILDING on Chaykin's experiments in panel arrangement, text-balloon placement, and parallel narration for over two decades now, and the thing still startles and disturbs the eye. It's like *Citizen Kane* in that way. Welles and Chaykin may not have invented or pioneered all the stylistic and technical innovations on display in their masterworks, but they were the first to put them all together in a way that changed how their successors thought about what they could and had to, and wanted to, do.

Citizen Kane remains an acknowledged influence on the movies and the comics that followed it. The debt to *American Flagg!*, while obvious, has been neglected. Its two great mid-eighties comics successors, Frank Miller's *The Dark Knight Returns* and *The Watchmen* by Alan Moore and Dave Gibbons, are hard to imagine without its example; those two books in turn influenced much that followed. *Flagg*, in both its style and its concepts, fed the literary genre of cyberpunk that has since watered the entire landscape of popular culture, from comics and computer games to movies to television programs. Again, I'm not arguing that Chaykin invented dystopian comics or cyberpunk, only that he articulated a set of tropes and "packaged" them in a way that brought them to durable, ravishing life.

If *American Flagg!* were merely influential or innovative, its relative retreat from view in the past two decades would be more understandable; the same goes for its oft-remarked effectiveness as prophecy. Accurate prediction of the future, of its technologies and traumas, has always seemed to me to be the least interesting thing about science fiction. So Arthur C. Clarke predicted the global satellite network—so what? He also predicted the widespread use of hovercrafts and the dominance by 2001 of the commercial Earth-Moon space trade by PanAm Airlines (d. 1991). Such prescience, or the obligation to display it is, more than bad writing, the element of a work of sf that most readily dooms it, regardless of whether the predictions turn out to be right or wrong. Every future we imagine is transformed inexorably into a part of our children's understanding of their past, of the assumptions their parents and grandparents could not help but make. If *American Flagg!* successfully predicted certain aspects of the hundred-ply world we live in now—and I think of it every time I see a lurid news headline about a pedophilic pop star crawl under breaking footage of carnage or disaster, while a network meat-puppet intones the latest official spin—than that very success would condemn it to seem, in time, eternally passé.

It is not, ultimately, the brilliance of its technique, or the aptness of the future it imagined that makes *American Flagg!* an enduring, necessary, and neglected pleasure, but the impeccable pop artisanship that produced it. So many of the purest pop masterpieces, from Michael Ritchie's *Smile* to Emmit Rhodes's self-titled first solo album, are neglected ones; even an acknowledged pop masterpiece like *Pet Sounds* has never quite shed its initial air of puzzlement-inducing letdown. *American Flagg!* has all the modern virtues that would seem to guarantee its place in the pantheon of seminal pop artifacts: irony, attitude, knowingness, cynicism, a familiarity with corruption and existential bad faith, a rapturous, at times hyperbolic sense of style, and that insatiable compulsion, mentioned earlier, to undercut. Its hero, Reuben Flagg, is not just a preening, self-regarding piece of beefcake—he's a redundant one, having been replaced, in his starring role on *Mark Thrust, Sexus Ranger*, by a hologram; and a self-conscious one. Nobody is more aware of the irony and implicit satire of his situation than Flagg. On the surface, he ought to be an ideal hero, and *American Flagg!* an ideal narrative, for our time.

But for all his cynicism and archness of eyebrow, Howard Chaykin, like so many pop artisans, draws the greatest part of his strength from the source that underlies all true visions of pop perfection: romance. Chaykin is, fundamentally, a romancer, "a storyteller," as the cliché has it, "in the grand tradition." Cynical, pompous or jaundiced, self-aware, embittered or corrupted, his heroes remain heroes, and the stories he tells never stray very far from their roots in Sabatini novels, *The Shadow* and *Doc Savage*, Chandler, Hammett, the films of Michael Curtiz. True friendship, true love, dying for a belief, self-sacrifice, even American ideals—such things, though he almost hates to admit it, are still possible in Chaykin's work. It's the instinct for popular narrative, for everything that Chaykin, in conversation, dismissively and affectionately terms "Pulp," that guarantees Chaykin's status as a true pop artisan, neglect and all. But it's that deep ambivalence toward romance, the need to undercut, that brings a problematic wobble to all of Chaykin's work. Like Paul Simon, who at once has felt and knows to be illusory the transcendent rapture of a killer hook, Chaykin's sense of romance and its conventions is always, at the same time, a sense of betrayal by them. In his earliest comics work drawing flashy, somewhat raw adaptations of Fritz Leiber's (already ironic) sword and sorcery tales, and creating short-lived titles such as *Iron Wolf* and *The Scorpion*, romance, the unabashed fabulating impulse of the storyteller, tended to win out. A cool head, quick reflexes, a steadfast purpose, and the love or memory of a good woman—along with that crucial Sabatinian "gift for laughter and a sense that the world was mad"—these were sufficient, or nearly so, to any challenge or evil the hero might encounter. In his recent work—though Chaykin's technique has attained the kind of effortless polish that, as with all experienced artists, is a synonym for correctly valuing his own strengths and weaknesses—the cynicism, the undercutting, and the mockery, revisionism, and satire have tended to gain the upper hand.

American Flagg! stands at the glorious midpoint, at that difficult fulcrum poised between innocence and experience, romance and disillusion, adventure and satire, the unashamedly commercial and the purely aesthetic, between the stoned, rangy funkiness of the seventies and the digitized cool of the present day, between a time when outrage was a moral position and a time when it has become a way of life. Such balancing acts have always been the greatest feats of American popular art; I hope these new editions of *American Flagg!* go a long way to establishing Howard Chaykin's place on the highest high wire. (2008)

D'Aulaires' Norse Myths, Ingri and Edgar Parin D'Aulaire

I WAS IN THE THIRD GRADE WHEN I FIRST READ THIS BOOK, and already suffering the changes, the horns, wings, and tusks that grow on your imagination when you thrive on a steady diet of myths and fairy tales. I had read its predecessor, *D'Aulaires' Book of Greek Myths* (1961), and I knew my Old Testament pretty well, from the Creation more or less down to Ruth. There was rape and murder in those other books, revenge, cannibalism, folly, madness, incest, and deceit. And I thought all that was great stuff. (Maybe that says something about me, or about eight-year-old boys generally. I don't really care either way.) Joseph's brothers, enslaving him to some Ishmaelites and then soaking his florid coat in animal blood to horrify their father: great stuff. Orpheus's head, torn off by a raving pack of women, continuing to sing as it floats down the Hebrus river to the sea: that was great stuff, too. Every splendor in those tales had its shadow, every blessing its curse. In those shadows and curses I first encountered the primal darkness of the world, in some of our earliest attempts to explain and understand it.

For whatever reason—call it the depravity natural to the young of our species—I was drawn to, and repelled by, that darkness. But even within the context of the stories, I knew that I was supposed to be only repelled by the darkness and also, somehow, to blame myself for it. Doom and decay, crime and folly, sin and punishment, the imperative to work and sweat and struggle and flee the Furies, these had entered the world with humankind: we brought them on ourselves. In the Bible it had all started out with a felicitous couple in the Garden of Eden; in the Greek myths, after a brief aeon of divine patricide and child-devouring and a couple of wars in Heaven, there came a long and peaceful Golden Age. In both cases, we were meant to understand, the world had begun with light and been spoiled. Thousands of years of moralizers, preceptors, drama-tists, hypocrites, and scolds had been at work on this material, with their dogma, and their hang-ups, and their refined sense of tragedy. The original darkness was still there in the stories, and it was still very dark indeed. But it had been engineered, like a fetid swamp by the Army Corps, rationalized, bricked up, rechanneled, given a dazzling white coat of cement. It had been turned to the advantage of people trying to make a point to recalcitrant listeners. What re-mained was a darkness that, while you recognized it in your own heart, obliged you at the same time to recognize its disadvantage, its impoliteness, its unacceptability, its being *wrong*, particularly for eight-year-old boys.

When Ingri and Edgar Parin D'Aulaire presented their version of the Greek myths for young readers, they kept the cannibalism, murder, revenge, folly, and deceit (soft-pedaling the rape, incest, and zoophilia), but, ever-faithful to their sources, they also kept (soft-pedaling, bless them) the moralizing, the fine calculus of punishment and retribution, the fundamental view that what I'm calling darkness—the tendency of our world toward calamity, violence, and ruin—arose with us, and is kept alive through our own untiring efforts at vanity and sin.

In the world of the Northmen, it was a different story.

As the D'Aulaires told it, in this follow-up volume to their *Book of Greek Myths* (originally titled *Norse Gods and Giants*), there was something in Scandinavian mythology that went beyond the universal appeal to an eight-year-old boy of violence, monstrosity, feats of arms, sibling rivalry, and ripping yarns. Here the darkness was not solely the fault of humans, the inevitable product of their unfitness, their inherent inferiority to the God or gods who—quite cruelly, under the circumstances—had created them.

The world of Norse gods and men and giants, which the D'Aulaires depicted, in a stunning series of lithographs, with such loving and whimsical and brutal delicacy, begins in darkness, and ends in darkness, and is veined like a fire with darkness that forks and branches. It is a world conjured *against* darkness, in its lee, so to speak; around a fire, in a camp at the edges of a continent-sized forest, under a sky black with snow clouds, with nothing to the north but nothingness and flickering ice. It assumes darkness, and its only conclusion is darkness (apart from a transparently tacked-on post-Christian postlude). Those veins of calamity and violence and ruin that structure it, like the forking of a fire or of the plot of a story, serve to make more vivid the magical glint of goodness that light and color represent. (Everything that is beautiful, in the Norse world, is something that glints: sparks from ringing hammers, stars, gold and gems, the Aurora borealis, tooled swords and helmets and armbands, fire, a woman's hair, wine and mead in a golden cup.) Here the gods themselves are no better nor worse, in the moral sense, than humans. They have the glint of courage, of truthfulness, loyalty, wit, and in them maybe it shines a little brighter, as their darkness throws deeper shadows. The morality encoded in these stories is a fundamental one of hospitality and revenge, gift giving and life taking, oaths sworn, dooms pronounced, cruel and unforgettable pranks. Moreover (and to my eight-year-old imagination this more than anything endeared them to me) the Norse gods are *mortal.* Sure, you probably knew that already, but think about it again for a minute or two. *Mortal gods.* Gods whose flaws of character—pride, unfaithfulness, cruelty, deception, seduction—while no worse than those of Jehovah or the Olympians, will one day, *and they know this,* prove their undoing.

Great stuff. Start anywhere; start with Odin. First he murders the gigantic, hideous monster who whelped his father, and slaughters him to make the universe. Then he plucks out his own right eyeball and trades it to an ice giant for a sip—a sip!—of water from the well of secret knowledge. Next he hangs himself, from a tree, for nine days and nine nights, and in a trance of divine asphyxia devises the runes. Then he opens a vein in his arm and lets his blood commingle with that of the worst (and most appealing) creature who ever lived, thus setting in motion the chain of events that will lead to the extinction of himself, everyone he loves, and all the nine worlds (beautifully mapped on the book's endpapers) that he himself once shaped from the skull, lungs, heart, bones, teeth, and blood of his grandfather.

The D'Aulaires captured all of this, reporting it in a straightforward, fustian-free, magical-realist prose that never stops to shake its head or gape at marvels and freaks and disasters, making them seem somehow all the stranger, and more believable. Their spectacular and quirky illustrations (a pair of adjectives appropriate to few illustrators that I can think of offhand) never found a more appropriate subject than the Norse world with its odd blend of gorgeousness and violence, its wild prodigies and grim humor. What makes the book such a powerful feat of visual storytelling is the way in which the prose and the pictures (reflecting, perhaps, the marriage and lifelong partnership of the authors) complement each other, advance each other's agenda. Every page that is not taken up by a giant bursting lithograph of stars and monsters is *ornamented* with a smaller drawing, or with one of the curious, cryptic, twisted little margin-men, those human curlicues of fire, that so disquieted me as a kid and continue, to this day, to freak out and delight my own kids. Through this intricate gallery of marvels and filigree the text walks with calm assurance, gazing calmly into every abyss, letting the art do the work of bedazzlement while seeing to it that the remarkable facts—the powers and shortcomings of Mjölnir the mighty hammer, the strange parentage of Sleipnir, Odin's eight-legged steed—are laid bare. This simultaneous effect of wonderment and acceptance, this doubled strength, allows the D'Aulaires to balance their re-creation of the Norse world exactly on its point of greatest intensity: the figure of Loki.

Ally and enemy, genius and failure, delightful and despicable, ridiculous and deadly, beautiful and hideous, hilarious and bitter, clever and foolish—Loki is the God of Nothing in Particular yet unmistakably of the ambiguous World Itself. It was in reading this book that I first felt the power of that ambiguity. Children start out with a morality that is the equivalent of scribbling, and in being taught to color inside the lines are rarely presented with literary characters who elude and evade those lines, falling at once within and without them. One never encountered Loki among the lists of Great Literary Heroes (or Villains) of Childhood, and yet he was my favorite character in the book that was for many years my favorite, a book whose subtitle might have been *How Loki Ruined the World and Made It Worth Talking About.* Loki was the god of the sloppily colored lineaments of my own childish mind, with its competing impulses of vandalism and vision, of imagining things and smashing them. And as he cooked up schemes and foiled them, fathered monsters and stymied them, helped forestall the end of things and hastened it, he was god of the endlessly complicating nature of plot, of storytelling itself.

I grew up in a time of mortal gods who knew, like Odin, that the world of marvels they had created was on the verge, through their own faithlessness and might, of Ragnarok, a time when the best impulses of men and the worst were laid bare in Mississippi and Vietnam, when the suburban Midgard where I grew up was threatened—or so we were told—by frost-giants and fire-giants sworn to destroy it. And I guess I saw all of that reflected in this book. But if those parallels were there, then so was Loki, and not merely in his treachery and his urge to scheme and spoil. Loki was funny—he made the other gods laugh. In his fickleness and his fertile imagination he even brought pleasure to Odin, who with all his well sipping and auto-asphyxiation knew too much ever to be otherwise amused. This was, in fact, the reason why Odin had taken the great, foredoomed step of making Loki his blood brother—for the pleasure, pure and simple, of his company. Loki was the god of the irresistible gag, the gratuitous punch line, the improvised, half-baked solution—the God of the Eight-Year-Old Boy—and like all great jokers and improvisers, as often the butt and the perpetrator of his greatest stunts. In the end, it was not the familiar darkness of the universe and of my human heart that bound me forever to this book and the Nine Worlds it contained. It was the bright thread of silliness, of mockery and self-mockery, of gods forced (repeatedly) to dress as women, and submit to the amorous attentions of stallions, and wrestle old ladies. The D'Aulaires' heterogeneous drawings caught hold precisely of that thread: they were pre-Raphaelite friezes as cartooned by Popeye's Elzie Segar, at once grandiose and goofy, in a way that reflected both the Norse universe—which begins, after all, with a cow, a great world-sized heifer, patiently, obsessively licking at a salty patch in the primal stew—and my own.

We all grew up—all of us, from the beginning—in a time of violence and invention, absurdity and Armageddon, prey and witness to the worst and the best in humanity, in a world ruined and made interesting by Loki. I took comfort, as a kid, in knowing that things had always been as awful and as wonderful as they were now, that the world was always on the edge of total destruction, even if, in Maryland in 1969, as today, it seemed a little more true than usual. (2005)

"The Rocket Man," Ray Bradbury

THE MOST IMPORTANT SHORT STORY IN MY LIFE AS A WRITER is Ray Bradbury's "The Rocket Man." I read it for the first time when I was ten. I was making my way, with pleasure, through a collection of Bradbury's stories called *R Is for Rocket*. I had been an avid reader for about five years, and at first the pleasure I felt was the familiar pleasure I derived from the flights of an author's fancy, and from the anticipation and surprise of plot. Then I came to "The Rocket Man." It's the narrative of the young son of a rocket pilot whose father is to him at once an ordinary, ordinarily absent father, puttering around the house on his days off, and a terrible, mysterious demigod whose kingdom is the stars. The danger of the father's profession, the imminence and immanence of death, lie upon the family like the dust of stars that the narrator lovingly collects from his father's flight suit every time the Rocket Man comes home. During one of the father's leaves, the family travels to Mexico by car. One evening they stop along a rural road to rest, and in the last light of the day the son notices bright butterflies, dozens of them, trapped and dying in the grille of the car.

I think it was when I got to the butterflies—in that brief, beautiful image comprising life, death, and technology—that the hair on the back of my neck began to stand on end. All at once, the pleasure I took in reading was altered irrevocably. Before now I had never noticed, somehow, that stories were made not of ideas or exciting twists of plot but of *language*. And not merely of pretty words and neat turns of phrase, but of systems of imagery, strategies of metaphor. "The Rocket Man" unfolds to its melancholy conclusion in a series of haunting images of light and darkness, of machinery and biology interlocked, of splendor and fragility. The sense of foreboding is powerful; the imagery becomes a kind of plot of its own, a shadow plot. The end, when it comes, is at once an awful surprise, and inevitable as any Rocket Man, or those who mourn him, could expect.

I have never since looked quite the same way at fathers, butterflies, science fiction, language, short stories, or the sun. (2002)

John Carter of Mars: Warlord of Mars, Marv Wolfman, Gil Kane et al.

IN 1950 RAY BRADBURY—ALONG WITH EDGAR RICE BURroughs, the greatest literary cartographer of the planet Mars—published a story called "The Exiles." It depicts the Sun's fourth planet as an unlikely home to the ghosts, witches, ghouls, vampires, and were-creatures of literature, along with the shades of their creators; a world where Poe rules over the Emerald City and Dickens wassails endlessly with Marley's ghost; all of them banished by a sterile, rationalist technocracy that sought to eradicate superstition and magic belief (even Santa Claus!) from the face of a future Earth. At the story's conclusion, astronauts from Earth decide to celebrate their conquest of the Red Planet by burning the last of their homeworld's forbidden tales of mystery and imagination. Thus, with a Halloween shriek, the world of romance dies away forever.

In fact, what came to pass, twenty-five years after "The Exiles," was precisely converse to Bradbury's tragicomic Martian fantasy. In 1975 a pair of probes, Vikings I and II, were launched from Earth, and soon after making planetfall began to transmit a dense stream of photographs and data. The detailed portrait that was subsequently built up of a world that, for millions of years, had been frigid, airless, waterless, barren, and altogether hellish, ought to have doomed, not Earth's phantom exiles, but the literary denizens of *Mars*. Not in an impromptu bibliopyre but one dry scoop of soil, one bleak video snapshot, one radio pulse at a time, the invaders from Earth ought to have eradicated, once and for all, every last Martian, red or green, who was ever set down in black-and-white.

Nineteen seventy-five was the year I discovered, and fell in love with, Barsoom. First in the Science Fiction Book Club's hardcover editions, each of which featured two of Burroughs's early Mars novels wrapped in a spectacular Frank Frazetta jacket, next in the complete Ballantine paperback series with their more staid yet still lovely Gino d'Achille cover art, and finally in the pages of the Marvel Comics title whose first issues, more than three decades after their first appearance, you now hold in your hands, I undertook a series of ever more rapt and dreaming excursions across the fifty-million-mile gulf of solar space to the ultimate planet of Romance. In the years since then, unlike Bradbury's earthly spooks, Barsoom (as the denizens of Burroughs's Mars call their harsh and arid yet beautiful and far from lifeless home) has proven immune to the tools and inferences of rational science. Probes come and go; robot rovers roll, and the resolution of the images of wasteland grows ever higher. And yet they live on: John Carter, Tars Tarkas, and the (always thus) incomparable Dejah Thoris; the ruined cities and still-mighty canals; the beasts and monsters who haunt the shores of long-dry seas.

Because I fear that, in this instance at least, the great Mr.

Bradbury—the writer who gave me my first everlasting lessons in literary style—missed, or chose to ignore, the true importance in the human imagination of the Ghost, the Witch, the Demon, the Monster, and all their shadowy brood. Like the Mars of planetary romance, such ideas in order to flourish do not require, nor do they necessarily find their most powerful expression in the service of literal belief. They exert their greatest power as *metaphors*—for guilt and regret, for uncontrollable sexuality, for psychological torment, for the violence of the natural world—and therefore they will endure and even thrive for as long as the chaos of nature and of human consciousness can be figured by them. Nature seems likely to hang on to her power to terrify humanity for a while yet, and as for the vaunted rational mind, the history of the modern era, from the Belgian Congo to Hiroshima, from Blake's satanic mills to the Pacific Trash Vortex, affords ample proof of rationalism's unbreakable connection to horror, destructiveness, torture, and all the novel monsters cooked up since 1750 or so by human genius; indeed, at its worst our civilization is itself rationalism's most monstrous, uncontrollable spawn.

The "true" literary Mars invented by Burroughs, working from mistaken clues first provided by the astronomer Percival Lowell, is a figuring of mortality, a metaphor for the fragility of life, and of the beauty to be found and the thrill to be derived from the acute consciousness thereof. This sharp, focused awareness of life's impermanence and fragility is a chief aim of wisdom, and it is the gaining of wisdom to which the true adventurer, often unintentionally, turns out to have dedicated himself, his wit, and his flashing blade. Mars, like us, lives to die. The magic space of adventure, as Paul Zweig notes in his marvelous study *The Adventurer* (1974), is a "strange distance," a space of "abrupt intensity" where death may, as nowhere else, be confronted, challenged, seen for what it is. Adventure and its literature never afforded a space more magical, a world where the precious fragility of life was more stark and apparent from one moment to the next, than Barsoom. Nothing we will ever learn about the soil and atmosphere of the dead, red iron rock next door can ever diminish Barsoom's savage charm.

In the post-Viking world of 1977, Marv Wolfman and Gil Kane and Dave Cockrum and I knew that. It was a knowledge reflected, as well, in the famous setting, "a long time ago in a galaxy far, far away" of a movie that premiered in the summer of that year, one which owed a considerable debt, in its spirit and particulars, to Burroughs's novels of Barsoom. For in the end all the planets of adventure, from Mongo to Tatooine to Pandora, are Mars; anyone seeking adventure beyond the terrestrial limits finds him- or herself, somehow or other, inexorably, on the planet of Burroughs, facing death in that strange distance, thrilled and grateful, once again, to have made the trip.

I recently came upon a manila folder containing many of my own literary productions from this time. It is carefully labeled, in three colors of felt-tip marker, MIKE "BURROUGHS" CHABON. (2011)

The Escapists, Brian K. Vaughan

ONE WEEKEND TOWARD THE END OF HIS PUBLIC LIFE, AS he and his ex-wife plied their yearly course along the circuit of comic book conventions, bickering, bantering, holding each other up when the sidewalks were icy or the stairs steep, Sam Clay found himself in Cleveland, Ohio, as a guest of honor at the 1986 ErieCon. ErieCon was a mid-sized regional show held in the ballroom of a Euclid Avenue hotel that stood, until it was demolished, across the street from a grand old movie palace that soon after also succumbed to the wrecking ball, during one of the spasms of redevelopment that have tormented Cleveland's slumber for the past forty years.

People who saw them making the con scene in those years were often touched by the steadfast way that Rosa Kavalier—born Rosa Luxemburg Saks in New York City in 1919 and known to the world, if at all, as Rose Saxon, a queen of the romance comics—kept hold of the elbow of one of her ex-husband's trademark loud blazers as they moved from curb to counter, from ballroom to elevator, from

bar to dining room. They were, people said, devoted to each other.
And undoubtedly this was the case. They had known each other for
more than forty-five years, and though no one ever quite untangled
the complicated narrative of their various creative and romantic
partnerships over the years, mutual devotion was certainly part of
the story. But the truth of the tight grip that Rosa kept on Sam was
that, after a series of unsuccessful operations to repair his damaged
retinas, the man could barely see a foot in front of his face.

"She's my seeing eye dog," he would say, and then he would
wait, wearing a shortsighted grin, as if daring his ex-wife to find no
humor in his witticism, a challenge she was always ready to accept.

But to the people who knew Sam—old-timers, friends, and en-
emies from the Golden and Silver Ages, the beaming young (or
formerly young) protégés who regularly radiated from the formless
warmth of the Kavalier-Clay ménage—it was obvious how humil-
iating he found his poor vision, his lousy teeth, the hobbled, foot-
dragging gait that had resulted from the surprise return, when he
hit his sixties, of the polio that crippled him as a boy. Sam Clay
was a professionally (if not always convincingly) fierce man whose
mighty shoulders and Popeye forearms attested to a lifelong regi-
men of push-ups, dumbbells, and the punching of speed bags. You
could see that he hated every moment he had to spend "hanging
around Rosa," in his own formulation, "like a persistent fart."

On this particular Saturday afternoon in Cleveland, Ohio, in
1986, therefore, when it came time for Sam to transfer custody, from
his plumbing system to the hotel's, of the Dr-Pepper-and-orange-
juice cocktail (mixed by a secret formula known to and palatable
only by him) which he had been swilling from a thermos all morning, Sam got up from the "Kavalier & Clay" table in Artist's Alley
and set forth alone to find the men's room, which, according to the
guy at the next table, lay just a few steps outside and to the left of the

Cuyahoga Ballroom's gilded doors. How hard could it be? Rosa was off somewhere having a confab with some skinny little thing named Diana from Comico, and Sam's new assistant Mark Morgenstern (later known for his work on the DC Vertigo revival of the old Pharaoh Comics title *Earthman*) was attending the Klaus Nordling tribute panel. And Sammy, Sam decided, could goddamn well find his own goddamn way to the toilet.

As it turned out, there was no bathroom just outside and to the left of the ballroom's gilded doors; or perhaps the ballroom had more doors than Sam knew about, or featured less gilding than he had been led to expect, or maybe, he thought bitterly, he was just so addled-pated and purblind that he no longer knew his left from his right. He spent ten minutes blundering around the elevator lobby, responding with cheerful irritation to greetings and good wishes from blurred faces and voices that sounded as though he ought to know them. But his attention was wholly occupied with the effort it cost him not to appear to be lost, blind, and in desperate need of a pee, so that he might as well have been in a crowd of strangers. There was an unpleasant incident with a large potted fern, and a compromising entanglement with the legs of a display easel. Sam's dignity—an attribute with which, until quite recently, he had never been unduly burdened—would not, it appeared, permit him to admit that he was in need of assistance.

At one point he found himself in an intimate, metallic space whose acoustics suggested a washroom or stall, and he knew a horrible instant of hope and relief before realizing that he was in fact riding an elevator. He got off at some floor and walked in some direction, trailing his right hand against the dark-red softness of the hallway's flocked wallpaper because once, many years before, in an issue of *Astounding*, he had read that you could always count on finding your way in and out of any labyrinth as long as, from the moment you entered it, you kept one hand in continuous contact with one wall. This expedient may, or may not, have had something to do with the fact that, twenty-five minutes after setting out from Artist's Alley full of piss and confidence, he succeeded, not without effort, in locking himself inside a broom closet.

Like most grave mistakes his became apparent more or less upon commission. The bright, burgundy, flocked-velvet blur of the hallway went black. The door shut behind him with the decisive click of some instrument of execution snapping to. There was an acrid bubblegum stink of disinfectant and the damp-bedsheet smell of old mop heads. Sammy knew a moment of pure infantile dread. Then in the darkness he smiled.

"At least," he pointed out to himself, unzipping his fly, "there'll be a bucket."

With a chiming like some liquid carillon he relieved himself into the rolling mop bucket whose contours his shoe tips then fingertips had revealed to him. Bliss, fulfillment through evacuation. He zipped up and began, with fresh dread, to contemplate the impossible task that lay before him, which consisted of shouldering the now almost unendurable and infinitely imperiled burden of his dignity while pounding on the door of the broom closet and screaming for help until he was hoarse, all the while enjoying the piscine bouquet of his own urine. He opened his mouth, ready to scream. Then he closed his mouth, experiencing second thoughts about this course. When, after all, they finally discovered his corpse, or perhaps his skeleton, in this closet, huddled over a bucket of ancient pee, that would perhaps be embarrassing for some people, but not for him, because he would be dead. He slapped the door once, twice with the flat of his hand. He leaned against a steel shelf stacked with rolls of toilet paper in their paper wrappers, and readied himself for the final indignity, and sighed.

There was a rattle—the doorknob—and then an insect scratching, wire feelers. And then a burst of light and air.

"I saw you go in," said a boy. "Then I heard knocking." A boy in a red baseball cap. An open mouth, maybe some kind of dirt around the mouth. Sammy leaned forward to get a better look. About ten years old, a standard-issue little American kid but with something sly in his eyes and an overall air of injury or grievance. He was wearing a red jersey with the word LIONS running in old-timey script across the front, and in his hand he held an open Swiss army knife. The grime on his lips a streak of chocolate, a chocolate crumb or two. A Hostess cupcake, or perhaps a Ding Dong.

"It smells kind of like pee in there," the boy said.

"God, you're right!" said Sam, waving his hand back and forth in front of his face. "This hotel really is a dump."

He stepped out of the closet and shut the door behind him.

"Hey, thanks, kid. Guess I—" But what was the point of lying? Would he ever see this kid again? Guess I just wandered into a closet. "Guess I had the wrong room. Thanks." He and the boy shook hands, the boy's boneless and reluctant in his. He gestured with his chin to the little red knife. "Pretty handy with that. What are you, the world's youngest second-story man? Hotel dick know about you?"

The boy blinked, as if doubting his own reply or the wisdom of even making it. His breathing came wheezy through congested nostrils.

"I'm an escape artist," the boy said at last, making it sound dull, offhand, disappointing, the way he might have said "I have a shellfish allergy."

"That so?" Sam felt his heart squeeze at the sound of the words "escape artist," the deviated-septum rasp, the eyes that sought to slip free of the enforced deadpan manner of a ten-year-old boy. "Good with locks?"

The kid shrugged.

"Yours was easy." The boy refolded the pick blade into his knife and returned it to the pocket of his jeans. "I'm actually not really all that good."

In his semi-blindness it took a moment for Sam to realize that the boy was crying, softly, and had been crying possibly for a long time before he took it upon himself to rescue the old guy in the closet.

"Hmm," he said. "So what are you doing, wandering around the hotel, freeing strange geezers from broom closets? Where are your mother and father?"

The kid shrugged.

"I'm supposed to be downstairs. At the league award lunch."

"You like baseball?"

Another shrug.

"I take it they aren't handing you any awards."

The boy reached into the pocket of his blue jeans again and took out a crumpled wad of paper. He handed it wordlessly to Sammy with an expression on his face of utter disdain for the paper and its contents. Sammy unfolded and smoothed it out and then pressed it right up to his right eye, the stronger, to read it.

"'Nice Try Citation,'" he said.

The boy leaned back against the far wall of the corridor and sank slowly to the ground until his forehead touched his knees.

"Long season?" Sammy said, after a moment.

"Ninth place," the boy said, his voice muffled and small. "Out of nine. Also I have personal problems I don't care to discuss."

Sam considered pressing but decided that when you were ten all your problems were more or less personal.

"Look at me," Sam said. "I just peed into a bucket."

This seemed to make the boy feel better about himself.

"Listen. I don't know what the trouble is. I'm going to, uh, respect your privacy there. But I appreciate your helping me. I'd like to pay you back." He reached into the hip pocket of his suit pants and then remembered that his wallet was in the breast pocket of his jacket, hanging over the back of the chair in Artist's Alley. "Only I'm, uh, busted." He rubbed at the stubble on his chin. "So I guess I need to find somebody else who's stuck in a jam, and do the same for them like you did for me. Creed of the League of the Golden Key."

"Huh?"

"Forget about it. What's your name?"

"Hey, dickhead!" A gang of boys, wearing red Lions jerseys and red caps tumbled into the hallway from the elevator and stood. "Vaughan!" The voice, cracking with mockery or pubescence, seemed to be issuing from the largest among them. "What the hell are you doing up here? Coach is looking everywhere for you! He called your mommy, dickhead!"

"You best get your ass downstairs!"

"Hey, Vaughan, who's the old guy?"

Sammy took a step toward the boy, Vaughan, and lowered his voice.

"They want to give you another certificate?"

"A trophy. But I saw mine. The head was missing. I guess maybe somebody, well. Broke it off. When I saw that, that's when I left."

"Come on, Vaughan!"

"Hey," Sam told the boys, flexing his Popeye arms, and putting as much Brooklyn into his voice as he could muster. It was, still, a decent amount. "Whyn't you punks get the hell out of here and leave the kid alone?"

The red mass hung a moment in the hallway, wavering like the afterimage of a bright flash on his damaged retinas. Then a moment later it was gone.

"You ever read comic books?" Sam asked the boy.

"Not really. Like, Archies?"

"Archies. No, well, Archie has his place. But—"

Sam reached a hand down and offered to help the boy to his feet.

"Look, they got a big show going on downstairs. Cuyahoga Ballroom. A comics show. You might like it. Take Doctor Strange. He's a magician. You'd like that one, I bet."

"I've heard of him."

"You ought to check it out."

He pulled the boy up and stepped away from him.

"I'd better get back to the banquet," the boy said.

"Suit yourself," Sam said. "'Suit yourself,' that's good advice. I wish somebody'd given it to me when I was your age."

They went to the elevator and the boy pressed the button. They said nothing when it arrived and the doors opened, and nothing until they were halfway down.

"'Suit yourself,'" the boy repeated. "I let you out of a dark, stinky closet where you could've died, you give me some cheap advice."

Sam looked at the boy and saw that sly light in the boy's eyes again.

"Ten-year-olds," Sam said, as he got out of the elevator at the Mezzanine. "God help me." The doors started to close on the boy and his chance to redeem himself and repay his debt of freedom. He stuck his arm in and stopped them from closing. "Check out the show," he said. "That's my advice to you. Cheap as it may be."

"I can't," the boy said. "I really don't think I can. But, uh, thanks."

"Vaughan. What's the rest of it?"

"Brian K. Vaughan." It came out in a rush, a single word, almost a single syllable.

"Uh huh. What's the K for?"

"Kellar."

"Like the magician. Self-Decapitation, right? Harry Kellar. That the guy?"

Brian K. Vaughan looked shocked, almost put out, as if his middle initial represented a grave and powerful mystery of which he had hitherto believed himself the sole initiate.

"Yeah," he said wonderingly.

Sam stepped back from the doors, and drew back his hand with a Harry Kellar flourish, and the door slid shut on Brian K. Vaughan who, having called home from a pay phone in the lobby, received permission to stay after the league banquet and attend the remainder of the Saturday session of ErieCon '86, at which he purchased a copy of *Strange Tales* number 146 (featuring Baron Mordo, Dormammu, and the Ancient One), in Very Good condition, thus altering the entire course of his future life, not to mention the lives of those of us who are fortunate enough to know and appreciate the comic book genius so wildly and thoroughly on display (along with the estimable talents of Steve Rolston, Jason Alexander, Philip Bond, and Eduardo Barreto) in the pages that follow.

He and Sam Clay never saw or spoke to each another again.

(2009)

Summerland

I.

I DID BELIEVE IN FAIRIES, I DID, I DID.

It started when I was eleven or twelve, around the time of my parents' separation, though at the time I would not have remarked, certainly, on the coincidence. It was just another plankton bloom of the imagination, nourished and steered by the currents of the books I was reading at the time: Katherine Briggs's *An Encyclopedia of Fairies*, Brian Froud and Alan Lee's *Faeries*, and collections of stories, like "Tam Lin" and "Thomas the Rhymer," about the Fair Folk and their ways, drawn for the most part from ballads and folk beliefs of the British Isles.

Moving along the 398s at the local branch of the Howard County (Maryland) Public Library, I soon discovered that all over Europe and around the world, in Russia, Japan, pre-Columbian North America, Appalachia, one found accounts of human dealings with diminutive beings who came from a hidden Other World with its own freakily nonhuman way of reckoning time and morality. There appeared to be surprising agreement, across many traditions, about certain behaviors common to these beings. They coveted human babies, for one thing, though they would kidnap anyone. If their victims escaped or were released from captivity in the Other World it would be as doddering old men and women who discovered that, in their world of origin, they had been gone for only a day; or who realized, encountering their own great-grandchildren, that a century had passed since their abduction. Around the world fairies and their analogs were said to often take the form of certain recurring animals—bears, black dogs, swans, cranes—or of long-haired women who stood in flowing robes along the shore of a lake, river, or sea, wailing, singing, and luring wayfarers to their deaths. It was said, all around the world, that you might bargain with these beings, or ward them off—often they were said to fear iron—but you could not hope for mercy from them, because they had no souls.

As the bloom spread its eddies in Julia sets across my twelve-year-old brain I decided that all this lore had a basis in reality, and that I believed in fairies.* I told myself this belief was a logical— and hardly original—inference given the universality and broad consensus of fairy reports in world culture.

This was a lie. I believed in fairies because I *wanted* to believe in fairies. A belief in fairies was something I cultivated, and concealed, not because of any preponderance of evidence but simply

---

* A conclusion that, needless to say, I kept to myself. God knew I already provided would-be tormentors with a visible enough target—thick eyeglasses repaired at one or both hinges by a hunk of black electrician's tape, conversant about Vulcan anthropology— without adding to it a sparkling coat of pixie dust. Even to pronounce the word "fairy" within earshot of certain individuals would be to dangerously echo and reinforce a judgment they had long since made about me.

because, for some reason, it gave me pleasure to do so. I slunk along the corridors of Ellicott City Middle School with my head down, eyes on the rubber toes of my Sears Jeepers, a fervent belief in fairies lodged secretly inside me like a tiny woodland scene tucked inside an Easter egg, a warming dram of whiskey hidden in the head of a walking stick.

This belief, like all our most fervent beliefs, was largely a matter of will. Even as a boy wandering hopefully into a ring of toadstools in the woods behind our house in suburban Maryland, I knew perfectly well that the magic circle of mushrooms had been sketched not by the nocturnal dancing of liminal creatures but by some peculiarity of fungal generation. To see the toadstool ring as a midnight dancing circle took *effort*. Believing in fairies was a kind of discipline, an enforced habit of looking and listening that invested the world around me with rich and strange possibility. Children, like scientists—and, at our best moments, like writers—know that the deepest mysteries are encountered when we are paying the closest attention. I hoped that if I kept my eyes on the shady green corners of my world I might, in due time, catch a glimpse, as through a rip in an invisible curtain, of a darting, gem-eyed, feral face.

2.

CHILDHOOD PASSED WITHOUT AFFORDING ME, DESPITE MY vigilance, any sighting or trace of elfin passage. In my attempts to explain this failure I entertained a number of theories. Perhaps fairies *had* existed at one time, working their mischief for long enough and over a geographical range wide enough to have lastingly permeated human memory, until the rise of modern industrial civilization had doomed them, or driven them permanently hence. Perhaps our world and faerie, as the Other World was often styled, were dimensions of reality that had overlapped for a few millennia before separating, Venn circles that no longer intersected, soap bubbles of space-time that had briefly kissed before drifting apart. Perhaps, as many had speculated, the elves, trolls, boggarts, kobolds, and other haunters of deep woods and wild places were the dwindled remnant of aboriginal pantheons, overthrown and superseded gods imbued by conquerors' guilt with the transferred resentment of the conquered who had worshipped them; or perhaps tales of fairies in their caves, barrows, and desolations represented the furtive presence, distorted and embroidered upon by centuries of human memory, of those conquered aboriginals themselves, lingering in their last retreats. Picts, say, or Neanderthals, or whatever Stone Age people the lonely Basques descended from, venturing forth now and then from remote redoubts or dark bogs to steal children, animals, and food.

As I grew into my teens, then, my belief cooled and shed an ever-dimmer light as it faded into a forlorn half-hope that fairies were something the world had lost, long before my belated appearance on the scene.* Their apparent total absence I saw as proof, or figuration, of all the glory that had passed and was always passing from the world. In my imagination fairies had shifted, as it were, from signified to signifier. Every time that happens, as Peter Pan explained to Wendy, there is a fairy somewhere that falls down dead.

---

* I confess—we might as well get it all out on the table—that at instants in my adult life the old belief returns, with abrupt and poignant force: a sudden snap of twigs (Robert Plant's "bustle in your hedgerow") while I was tramping across a field near Avebury, a fleeting glint of silver among the shadows under a stand of ancient redwoods outside Ukiah, and the heart leaps. Such moments are rare, however, and the old habit of paying attention, of watching the shadowy corners of the world, has been yoked to more humdrum ends.

3.

I WAS BORN NEAR SUNSET, AND FOR AS LONG AS I CAN REMEM-
ber have been liable to feelings of belatedness, of having shown up
just as light and fire were fading from the sky. Among my very earliest memories is one of gold-banded panatelas and perfectos ranged
in ornate boxes on the shelves of a glass counter in the lobby of
Ricardo's Mexican restaurant in Phoenix, Arizona; and of knowing, without knowing how I knew, that during some vanished Age
of Cigars such counters had once been commonplace in restaurant
lobbies, and that this particular one, beside the Kiwanis Club gum-
ball machine, was already, in 1966, among the last of its kind. As
my hatless father waited for his change at the cash register I held on
to his hand, staring into the case, awash in regret for a world and a
time—of cigars, fedoras, Indian-head nickels—that I had somehow
managed to lose without ever first possessing.

In such feelings of inherited loss there is nothing unique, to me
or to my generation of Americans, even though the America that we
inherited—or so we have been constantly reminded, by both Right
and Left, all our lives—was something poisoned, debased, frag-
mented, brutalized, commodified, fallen from the grace of God, dis-
tanced irretrievably from the Puritan work ethic, from small-town
values, from egalitarian principles, from the can-do spirit that had
rid the world of polio and fought wars for just causes against un-
ambiguous foes, and from the shucks-ma'am Gary Cooper brand of
excellence that would never step back, at the plate, to admire a home
run shot sent arcing over the left-field wall into the stands. To come
into consciousness of the world as a site of perpetually vanishing
glory—of promise squandered, paradise spoiled, utopia unachieved—
is and has always been the inheritance of every American, as the
famous closing paragraphs of *The Great Gatsby* make clear.

Nor is this sense of belatedness—the narrator of *The Amazing Adventures of Kavalier & Clay*, a bit dismissively, calls it "the aetataureate delusion"—unique to Americans; it underlies, and renders enduringly poignant, all accounts of Golden Ages, of primal innocence and of paradise lost, going back as far as the earliest books we have: to Gilgamesh and the opening chapters of Genesis.

Perhaps the sense of belatedness is an artifact or hangover of the evolution of consciousness itself, of the descent of homo sapiens from the smooth, continuous flow of animal time into human time, discontinuous and pulsing like a watch-works with the awareness of mortality. Perhaps a child or grandchild of the first hominid to abandon the forest canopy for the forest floor looked up, one ancient African evening, at the sunlight that was fading in the treetops overhead, and felt just the way I felt when I saw those El Productos in their gaudy boxes.

4.

IN THE FALL OF 2000, AROUND THE TIME THAT *Kavalier & Clay* was published, motivated in part by the desire to try something different after the long, dense slog of writing that book, and in part by the experience of a family car trip spent listening to Jim Dale's thrilling recording of the first Harry Potter, I determined to write a novel that would be set in an "American faerie," an idea that had been lying in a dusty alcove of my imagination for at least twenty-five years.*

That, at least, is the account of *Summerland*'s genesis that I have

---

* Since about 1976, i.e., around the heart of the years I spent trying as hard as I could, through the smudged lenses of my taped-up glasses, to see fairies in the leafier corners of the Baltimore-Washington Corridor.

always given until now. Usually I have added that, after I became a father and began reading aloud to my children, hoping to make readers of them, I started looking for a good novel to read to them about baseball, hoping also to make them into baseball fans. While many fine and even wonderful baseball novels continued to be written for adults, however, the total number of fine or even semi-decent baseball novels written for children since my own boyhood seemed, when I looked around, to have remained mysteriously equal to the total number of Chicago Cubs World Series appearances since 1945.

When I decide to write a book, my explanation would continue—this is a line I've used a lot of times, over the years, and not just to account for the existence of *Summerland*—it's because there seems to be a small gap in the stacks, right about where you might want to shelve a hard-boiled Jewish detective novel of alternate history, say, or a novel set during the Golden Age of American comic books, or a somewhat-better-than-semi-decent baseball novel for children. This apparent gap, along with the lingering pleasurable effects of Dale's Rowling and the hope that writing for younger readers would not only make for a nice change but might also, perhaps, take some of the inevitable pressure off *Kavalier & Clay*'s successor, settled the matter.

Nearly a decade and a half on, I can see that my standard account of *Summerland*'s origins, while superficially factual and sincerely intended, doesn't explain anything. The lingering pleasure of my immersion into Jim Dale's voice and J. K. Rowling's world does not explain why, at the end of that summer of 2000, I found myself digging up and dusting off a fragmentary idea, conceived by a thirteen-year-old, Vulcan-studying fairy-believer with amblyopia, for a book that populated latter-day America with fairies. And a near-total absence of good baseball novels for children truly does not explain why I felt that I ought to write a baseball novel about *fairies*, since any better-than-semi-decent baseball novel for children, even one completely devoid of fairies, would presumably have done the trick.

My standard account also fails to explain why, having settled on this odd cocktail of subject matter, I didn't write a book that deployed fantasy elements within the cozy confines of a familiar template, using the tropes and conventions of juvenile sports fiction the way Rowling had used the template of the classic British public-school novel (*Ethan Feld and the Other-World Series?*); or, conversely, why I didn't write a pastoral, Millhauser-like baseball fairy tale about, say, a brilliant young phenom abducted into Elfland who teaches its denizens the ways of baseball (*The Elves of Summer?*).

Instead, I decided to make *Summerland* a work of epic fantasy, a quest novel set against a backdrop of existential conflict between good and evil in a "secondary creation" (to employ the term preferred by J.R.R. Tolkien) derived from a preexisting mythology, inspired by the examples of Tolkien, C. S. Lewis, Lloyd Alexander, and, in particular, of Susan Cooper in her *The Dark Is Rising* sequence of novels, childhood favorites of mine, which blended a familiar, contemporary (but never cozy) reality with Arthurian material in a way that captured, like few other modern works of fantasy, the uncanny, disturbing nature of faerie.*

This kind of explanatory failure is routine with me and, I imagine, far more common among writers than they tend to acknowledge or that their readers tend to understand. If you publish a novel, and if people read it, it's usually not too long before some of those people start asking you, like the parents of a teenaged

---

* It was not yet apparent, at the time, at least not to me, that Rowling's ambition in the Potter series would turn out to be similarly grand, and dark.

shoplifter caught wearing a brand-new pair of sneakers, where you got it. The problem, at least in my case, is that most of the time, and certainly in the period immediately following a book's completion, the only truly honest reply to such a question happens to be a phrase that I have always found to be among the hardest, of all phrases, to utter: "I don't know."

I have confessed elsewhere to the shame and frustration of my lifelong struggle against being a know-it-all, a struggle in which, one imagines, the words *I don't know* might at times prove to be of some use. But there it is: "I don't know" is not a congenial place for me, especially when called to account for my work by readers. I want to be helpful. I want to satisfy, even to please. I want to show that I have been paying attention. And, really—how can you work on a novel every day for a year, three years, five years, *and not know how it began?* To admit that would be like confessing that I don't remember how my wife and I met (blind date, Savoy restaurant, NYC, 5/9/1992).

The main reason that I resist professing my ignorance of a novel's true point of origin, however, is my distaste for the way that when writers talk about writing—I'm as guilty of this as anyone—we so often indulge in what feels like a deliberate practice of mystification. *The whole book just came to me, like a vision, complete.* Or, *I was inexplicably haunted by the image of an older man, a teacher I thought, watching a younger man, his student, standing outside in the rain with a gun to his head.*[*] Or that perennial favorite *It was like someone else was doing the talking. I was just taking dictation.* Every time that happens there is a fairy, somewhere, that rolls its eyes.

So when people ask me to explain how I came to write a book, because I am a know-it-all, and because I am at pains to avoid

---

[*] Pure B.S.

suggesting that I believe the sources of our ideas and inspirations lie beyond human understanding, perhaps in the mysteries of the Jungian unconscious, I can never bring myself to say, "I just really don't know."

A better response, as it turns out, and one that I intend to try next time, might be *How about asking me again in fifteen years?* Because looking back, now, at the birth of *Summerland,* it seems fairly obvious why I wrote an epic fantasy novel about baseball and fairies: as a direct response to the experience of overwhelming loss.

5.

JUST AS THE MAJOR LEAGUE BASEBALL SEASON OF 2000 WAS getting under way, about six months before I first began to imagine the contours of the novel that would become *Summerland,* my wife and I were informed of an ambiguous but possibly grave abnormality in the genes of the child she had then been carrying for seventeen weeks; an incipient boy whom we had taken to calling Rocketship,* at the suggestion of his future older brother, then two and a half.

The pregnancy had been unplanned and with our crowded lives already dominated, even swamped, by the work of rearing the two children we already had, was not, at first, entirely welcome. After four months, however, the sheer habit of joyful expectancy formed the first two times around had softened if not entirely allayed our anxiety. With the baby's growing presence easily inferred from the considerable swell of my wife's third-time belly, the four of us had

---

* The fetus was also sometimes known, per another brotherly suggestion, as Nubakaduba.

begun to prepare a place for Rocketship and his little story in the overarching narrative of our family, like people on a sofa sliding over to let another person sit down.

I remember that I buried myself deeply in baseball that season, which culminated with my team, the San Francisco Giants, winning their division, then losing the National League pennant in a sweep to the Mets. I was already a devoted Giants fan and a lifelong lover of baseball, but that season I watched every game the Giants played, in the stands of their perfect new ballpark or on television. When I could not watch I would listen on the radio. If the Giants had the day off, I took in another game—the Devil Rays, the Brewers, I didn't care. I took out a subscription to *Baseball America*, so that I could keep apprised of events and portents down on the farm teams, and pored every morning over the box scores.

All this deep immersion into the baseball season of 2000 was not intended to help me take my mind off the fact that my wife and I had terminated her pregnancy, to keep me from dwelling on the loss of that baby and on the space that we had made for him and his story in our lives; on the contrary. A father, it seemed to me in those months, had one essential job: to protect his children against harm. In that one job I had failed. I did not try—I could not hope—to escape the contemplation of my failure. And the longer I contemplated it, the more steadily baseball returned my gaze; the more eagerly baseball seemed to rise to meet the daily aching in my chest.

"It breaks your heart," as the opening sentence of A. Bartlett Giamatti's baseball lamentation "The Green Fields of the Mind" famously declares. "It is designed to break your heart." The notorious sentimentality of twentieth-century Red Sox fans notwithstanding, Giamatti had it right. As has often been observed, baseball makes legends out of hitters who fail, over the course of their careers, nearly seventy percent of the time. A single run, a single hit, a lousy passed

ball, can ruin the masterwork of a pitcher's afternoon. So congenial
to loss is the game of baseball that a team who lose almost as many
games as they win can take a division, as the San Diego Padres did
in 2005.* Baseball was not my means of escape in the summer of
2000; it was my support group. Baseball understood.

When *Summerland* begins, the father of its protagonist, Ethan
Feld, has already failed Ethan in the clutch, having been powerless
to protect the boy from the loss of his mother. Over the course of
the book, partly out of shame over that powerlessness, but also for
all the usual fatherly reasons—overwork, mental abstraction, in-
ability to communicate love and tenderness—Mr. Feld withdraws
into his failure, haunted by it like a snake-bit hitter going 0 for 20.
At last he becomes so immured that he is transformed into something quite horrible (I remember seriously spooking myself when I
wrote those passages). I did not want that to happen to me and the
two living, growing, watching, listening, waiting, wondering children who squeezed up against me on the couch in the living room
every night, one on each side, trying to figure out what it was about
their father that would make him want to sit there scowling back
at the Giants' pitcher—killed the next year when his car collided
with a tractor—as the poor man fell behind in the count with the
bases loaded and, with the next pitch, earned himself a demotion
to Fresno.

With my children over the course of that season, like a hitter
scuffling at the plate, I struggled, every day, to connect. It was inevitable, I suppose, that I should begin to consider trying to do so
in the form of a story; isn't that, after all, what stories are for? Inevitable, too, perhaps, that the story assembling itself in my imagination seemed to want to play itself out on a baseball diamond.

---

* With a record of 82–80.

6.

BASEBALL AS WE KNOW IT WAS CODIFIED AND POPULARIZED IN the United States just as the balance was tipping forever from the rural and agrarian to the urban and industrialized; it came of age as a national game during the Civil War, disseminated by city-boy soldiers from New York and Massachusetts, often played across enemy lines on the rolling green battlefields of summer. Within walls and grandstands of brick and steel—like the case filled with cigars, resplendent in their boxes, that gave me an early taste of belatedness—ballparks have always seemed to enclose, and thus to preserve, the bright grass and golden dirt of some lost arcadia.

The sense of loss enfolded within the confines of a ballpark is not a passing wave of poignancy, a wistful pang of nostalgia between beer ads or flats of curly fries. It reproaches us, the way the dead reproach us in our dreams. Ghosts of the great ones and the vanished "glory of their times," as Lawrence Ritter titled his seminal oral history of baseball's mythic era, haunt the outfield and the basepaths*—all those titans and paladins and outsized bravos of tall tales, beside whom the current nine are always nothing but a bunch of overgrown boys and worn-out men with crafty eyes and paunches. With its grass and sky and lazy distances, a ballpark itself haunts its neighborhood, even after it has been torn down, surrounded, or swallowed up by a city that is, like all cities, a failure, a falling away from the Heavenly Jerusalem. Tucked into a city's secret green pocket, lonely as the Lorax's last truffula tree, a ballpark is an endless green reproach, seconded by ghosts and legends, for

---

* The first organized game of baseball was played in Hoboken, New Jersey, in 1846, at a park fittingly called Elysian Fields.

our collective failure to deserve them, and a constant reminder of the loss of something we never really had.

As I scuffled and scratched my way, that summer, toward the story I hoped was going to help me connect with my children, it may have been this constant sense of reproach, of being haunted by the loss of something never possessed, that sent me to that dusty alcove of my writerly memory, where I stumbled across that long-abandoned project for a novel set in an American faerie. Did I feel a weird thrill of recognition as I uncovered it, a sense of time collapsing on itself? I had first conceived it, after all, at the time or in the immediate aftermath of my parents' divorce, that event which, until April 2000, had for so long held the title of Worst Moment In My Entire Life.

The period of my belief in fairies, as I've said, coincided almost exactly with the years in which my parents were busy adding their marriage, and my family as I had known it, to the world's august and sorry tally of lost things. Like many children of divorce I had experienced the failure of my parents' marriage as my own. As with the elf-knot that snarled Rocketship's DNA, I had failed to do the impossible thing that might have prevented it. At both times—in 1976 and in 2000—hoping to understand, cope with and transform calamity into narrative, my thoughts appear to have turned to the lore of fairies. I think that now I understand why.

Long before we have the power or the opportunity to give offense to it, the world has already set itself against us. We are like the occupiers of a battered fortress abandoned by an enemy who, before retreating, took care to salt the grounds with mines and rig the rooms and corridors with booby traps. Fairies, the remnant of a departed grandeur, a fallen race, a regretted creation, help to explain the way the world that has been left to us so often feels hostile to our presence.

In the tricks and mischief they delight in playing—souring our milk, tangling our horses' manes, captivating our spouses, blighting our infants—fairies embody the experience of living in a world that we have been obliged, even though someone else broke it, to buy. Fairies were here first. They had the world, and lost it. Now, in their ruin, they try to ruin what they can. They are the secret hostility that haunts creation like Tolkien's barrow-wights among the rubble of fallen Arnor.

It was this Tolkienesque duality in my lifelong sense of belatedness, the way there always seemed to be something both poetic and inimical in my inheritance, the way lost things had the power both to haunt and to exalt, to move and to reproach, that steered the book I decided to write, about fairies and baseball, toward epic fantasy. Epic fantasy is the literature of our innate consciousness that we have inherited a world in ruins. *The Lord of the Rings* is a record, finally, not of the destruction of the One Ring in the fires of Mordor but of the departure of the Elves, and thus of magic, from the world. That story, though I did not really believe in elves, had always struck me as fundamentally true; at any rate it helped to explain the sense of loss that appeared, from earliest childhood, to be my patrimony.

I did believe in magic, the magic I learned at the hands of Tolkien and Cooper and Alexander, Louise Fitzhugh, Ursula K. Leguin, E. L. Konigsberg—all the wizards and enchantresses who cast their spells over me as child. It was the kind of magic that, at least while you remained between the covers of a book, could bind up and repair all the cracks in the world, relight the lamps, restore what had been lost, heal what had been broken. Of course, it was only sleight of hand, a trick of ink on paper. But it was better than nothing; it was better, really, than almost anything else.

I began to write the book that became *Summerland,* which

includes, in addition to the story of Mr. Feld's redemption, a lost little fairy boy named Nubakaduba, and it was not very long (a year or so, about as quickly as I've ever managed) before I arrived at the book's final pages. There I found, at least while I was writing them, a measure of genuine solace, as I circled the bases with Ethan Feld on the field at Applelawn, and broke the window of heaven. I hope that old readers have found and new ones will find a little solace of their own, between its covers, for all that they may have lost. If not, then I hope they find it elsewhere. As for the children to whom the book is dedicated, and for whom it was written—four of them, in total, by the time my wife and I were through—I'm sure they'll get around to reading it one of these days. I know they know that, like their father, it's always there for them when they need it. (2002)

Fountain City, excerpt

I WAS LOST. FOR A COUPLE OF YEARS I HAD DREAMED A LONG and private dream about Pittsburgh and the mysteries of summertime, but now, as if by means of some pulp-madman ray gun, the solitary dream had escaped my head. Recently, by the strange alchemy of a judge's words acting upon our own stubborn refusal to swerve at the last minute (how poignant and sweet, already, was the memory of the night on which we briefly decided to call the thing off!), my new wife and I had avowed our poor judgment under the gaze of our loved ones and the state of Washington, in a ceremony that itself unfolded with the mistaken inexorableness of a dream. Now, a few days later, our honeymoon bed in a hotel in Venice was a place of operatic vastation and woe. I was twenty-four, rootless, feckless, homeless, and mapless; a child of divorce; raised in the broken Utopias of the 1970s and Columbia, Maryland. I stood in a narrow *ruga* somewhere in the Cannaregio, *solo, abbandonato, perduto,* briefly and prefiguratively separated from my bride (we would separate in earnest, for the first time, later that fall), baffled, literally not knowing which way to turn.

That was when I saw the mirage. It hovered, small, golden, rectangular, in a shop window, adorned, in modest serif type, with a question that felt inexplicably pertinent at that moment: *What Is Post-Modernism?*

I went into the bookshop and asked to have a look at the book. I flipped through its pages as if searching for a clue, a way home, a cool drink for a thirsty soul. The first thing that caught my eye seemed, in the way of all mirages, to promise all that. It was a reproduction of a watercolor painting by Leon Krier, an architect famed for his unrealized visions of ideal cities, depicting a place that might have been Washington, D.C., or Washington as it might have been, if the original baroque urban plan, as devised by Pierre L'Enfant, had been realized. It offered a bird's or rather aeronaut's view of that imaginary city, placing the spectator above and slightly to the right of an old-fashioned propeller plane whose wing was dipped in playful farewell, implying that this more perfect capital was receding beneath one as one left it behind. The colors—green boulevards, blue tidal basin, white monuments—were at once intense and wistful, as if the picture were not even a view at all but a recollection: the memory of a place that never was.

I was born in Washington, and raised in the "planned community" of Columbia, Maryland, a city that, like my birthplace, had first existed as a prediction, a grandiose diagram of itself when at last perfected. Washington's plan and Columbia's were always linked in my mind, not only by their primal nature as idealized, impossible map-selves but also by the mythic presence throughout my childhood of the enigmatic black astronomer, inventor, and surveyor Benjamin Banneker, who lived somewhere in the vicinity of Columbia during the late eighteenth and early nineteenth centuries and who,

according to legend, had reconstructed L'Enfant's drawings from
memory after the intemperate Frenchman stormed off the job in
a Frenchman-like huff. As with Washington, D.C., however—and
like the doomed novel that now, in that Venetian bookstore, began
to kindle in my mind—Columbia was never to know completion,
at least in the form its original planners so fervently imagined.
Columbia was a dream, too; a Great Society, "Kumbaya" dream of
racial equality and ecumenical coexistence, open space and open
classrooms, and I dreamed it for eleven years. But Columbia had
fallen short of its projections, my parents had divorced, and we all
abandoned Columbia, for California or the decidedly non-Kumbaya
city of Pittsburgh. Yet it was not until I saw that little painting by
Leon Krier on page 20 of *What Is Post-Modernism?,* and caught a half-
remembered glimpse of a never-was city, that I understood, truly
felt, the loss of home: that endless, ongoing sense of longing for a
place that never quite came into being, which is the answer, finally,
to the question posed by the title of Charles Jencks's book.

When I returned home from that honeymoon trip I did some
research into the work of Leon Krier, and began to imagine writing a novel about a grieving or at least poetically sad young man
who apprenticed himself to a visionary, postmodern architect out
of a longing for some vanished home or notion of home. That was
all I began with. Over the course of the next half decade I wrote
fifteen hundred pages and incorporated into the plot and fabric of
the novel everything from messianic Zionism to French cuisine
to radical environmental activism. And baseball. Oh, and Japa-
nese monster movies. But when at last I abandoned work on the
damn thing, stepping out on it to begin what became *Wonder Boys,*
that was still, in some way, all that I had: the lost kid and the illusory vision of home. If only, I have since often thought, I could
have found some way of being truer, of hewing closer, to that kid

and that longing—in fewer than, say, four hundred pages. If only I possessed whatever was required to finish that book, to redeem that lost promise, to finish what I had begun. If only I could have found, to paraphrase Beckett, a better way to fail.

Because I believe in failure; only failure rings true. Success is an aberration, a random instance devoid of meaning. The extraction from my head of the summertime Pittsburgh novel by the dream-thieving ray of the New York Publishing Entity, and its subsequent "successful" publication, taught me nothing useful about the world, nothing (apart from some fresh lessons in my own vanity) that felt remotely useful to understanding myself, that floundering, tempo-rizing, procrastinating, rationalizing, frequently inert waster of time.

Furthermore, as with the scientist, the chef, the parent, as with anyone caught up in the practice of art—that distillation of the human enterprise, which is, at its simplest, a business of paying attention—failure instructs the writer. Every novel, in the mo-ments before we begin to write it, is potentially the greatest, the most beautiful or thrilling ever written; but in the long dying fall *after* we have finished it (if we finish it), every novel affords us, with the generosity of a buffalo carcass affording meat, hide, bone, horn, and fat, the opportunity to measure precisely, at our leisure, the distance between it and that L'Enfant-esque dream. Our greatest duty as artists and as humans is to pay attention to our failures, to break them down, study the tapes, conduct the postmortem, pore over the findings; to learn from our mistakes.

And so for a long time after that novel failed I tried, as nature fitted me to do, to extract some valuable lesson, some use, from the failure of *Fountain City*:

1. Write smaller books. *Fountain City* took place on three continents, in two cities (one fictional), over a long period, with an omni-

scient narrator, and featured numerous characters and settings. *Wonder Boys,* my first novel, took place in sweet, little old Pittsburgh, with a small cast of characters, over an even narrower scope of time: a single weekend.

This lesson was ignored in favor, and failed to stand up to the example, of *The Amazing Adventures of Kavalier & Clay,* and so I subsequently discarded it for:

2. Trust your gut. I had known fairly soon after beginning work on the book, within the first twelve to eighteen months, that something about it was, in the technical parlance of writers, fucked. My hero was too passive. His grief was too vague. I knew nothing about how architects really worked and yet was, myself, too passive to figure out how to remedy my ignorance. Et cetera. Often when I sat down to work I would feel a cold hand take hold of something inside my belly and refuse to let go. It was the Hand of Dread. I ought to have heeded its grasp.

But I had taken a sizable advance for *Fountain City* from the publisher of my first novel. If I abandoned the book, I worried, I might have to repay that money. I might fall prey to the black arts of lawyers. On the other hand, I used to worry, sitting down to try to render less vague my protagonist or less germane my ignorance of the practice of architecture, what if the only reason that I daily persevered, in spite of my regular massage sessions under the Hand of Dread, was fear, mere financial panic? How could such a motive possibly be the healthy basis for artistic creation? Clearly, therefore, when *Fountain City* failed, the lesson of that failure was:

3. Don't take advances; sell your work only when it is complete. A monetary obligation to one's publisher placed all kinds of un-

due pressure, both subtle and overt, on the writer, chief among them the aforementioned pressure to persist on a fucked project well beyond the point of reason. The pressure of an advance put the writer into the frame of mind that kept a nation, for example, after vast expenditure of moral, human, and financial treasure, fighting a war for years beyond even the most delusive hope of victory. And yet writers needed money, the same as everyone else, and when it became available they were no less likely than anybody else to take it. If you had a family to support, and hoped to buy not only food, clothing, and Polly Pocket So Hip Cruise Ship play sets, but also some time in which actually to *write* novels, refusing to take advances meant you had to be wealthier, more optimistic, stronger-willed, or far better at managing your time than most of the writers I knew. Therefore:

4. Persevere. Because in later years, as I worked first on *The Amazing Adventures of Kavalier & Clay* and then on *The Yiddish Policemen's Union*, for both of which I accepted generous advances from publishers, the Hand of Dread returned, many, many times, to entwine its chill fingers among my inward organs. Many times while writing those books, I felt myself overwhelmed with panic, doubt, a certainty of failure. If I had chosen to learn from lesson 1, I would have laid both books aside before I wasted as much time on them as I had on *Fountain City*. And yet I had stumbled onward, written myself around or through or out of my doubt and difficulty, finishing the books as well as I could manage to finish them, and moving on to the next.

Just before I finally gave up the effort to find the lesson in the disaster of *Fountain City*, to see in it what Richard Sennett, in his lovely study *The Craftsman*, calls a "salutary failure," I produced the annotations that follow this preface. After an absence of several years, I dove back down to the wrecked book I had abandoned at the sea-bottom of my hard drive, to see what treasure, if any, I might hoist up. What I found, more than any salutary wisdom, was a strangely intact record of my life during the time I was writing the book, a bubble of ancient air trapped in the caulked hull of the sunken novel. Neighbors, arguments with my ex-wife, meals eaten, hostels haunted, shoes I used to have, all had made their way into the book, invisibly and unknown as such to anyone but me. I also found all kinds of bits and pieces of my childhood and life before my work on the novel began, stories and anecdotes and people and settings that, having served nobly and without complaint to feed the needs of the failed novel, receded or vanished completely from my own lived memory, until I rediscovered them, touched by the reunion, in the pages of *Fountain City*.

As I began to adumbrate, by means of numbered notes, this idea of a "life in the margins," I also found myself following and uncovering traces of the mysterious life of a book, any book, the history of its birth, growth, evolution, and—in this instance—its untimely death. Believing fervently as I do that nothing succeeds like failure, I hoped to dig up, and to share, like a special commission appointed by Congress to investigate some disaster, the lessons of the wreck of *Fountain City*, in the hope that others might learn from, and thus receive the salutary benefit of, my mistakes. But then other, more pressing obligations intruded before I could produce annotations for more than the first four chapters, and the great brined and barnacled hulk sank back to the silence and dark, and so in that effort, too, as in so many others before and since an afternoon in Venice twenty-three years ago, when I foolishly thought I knew everything there was to know about being lost, I failed. (2010)

OUTROS

Fountain City, excerpt

IT GOES ON LIKE THAT FOR QUITE SOME TIME, FROM PARIS TO
Florida, from sorrow to rapture, from miscue to false step, and now
even the annotations themselves have, like the apparatus and tackle
of some failed salvage operation, become encrusted with disuse and
hold within them the evocative air of the time when I sent them
unreeling down into the depths.

Reading through these chapters once again to prepare them for
publication, mildly alert for typos, all hope of deriving some helpful lesson from them long since exhausted, I confess that I found
myself grooving on them, just a little bit, here and there. And when
I came to the end of this little sample I felt toward them the surprising stirring of what I might call a sense of fruitful incomple-
tion, a desire, or at least a wish, that this book might, after all, have
been steered to its intended destination. Surely, I thought, if I show
these chapters to my wife, she would be able to figure out what parts
of the story needed to be weeded or whacked into alignment—

And that was the moment that I realized, after eighteen years, what went wrong with *Fountain City*. I understood, at last, the lesson to be drawn from this disaster, the finding of my investigatory committee:

Marry a strong, talented, vocal, articulate, and above all persuasive reader.

The Mysteries of Pittsburgh was written while I was in the MFA program at UC Irvine, and it had plenty of readers among my teachers and workshop-mates, many of them readers who were strong, talented, et cetera, sensitive alike to the corn and the bullshit in my language, the flaws and the untapped resources in my story construction, the overlong and the overhasty, the useless and the underexploited. But for one reason and another, some marital, some personal, some just the breaks, I wrote *Fountain City* pretty much alone. I had an editor and an agent, and they generously gave me their notes and support and intelligent suggestions, but I didn't have anyone leaning on me, the way a good workshop leans on you, steadily, consistently, even daily, so that ultimately leaning becomes indistinguishable from holding you upright.

By the time I met Ayelet Waldman, it seemed to be too late. I was sick of the damn book beyond any hope of leaning or support. And yet in the years that followed, as I wrote other books, Ayelet managed to drag, hoist, cajole, or lure me across many such dread-filled patches, through many months during which I and my lame-ass novel, any of my lame-ass novels, felt fucked. But now I see that the reason Ayelet failed to pull off this feat that very first time, when, as my new girlfriend, she read what was to be the last complete draft of *Fountain City*, was not because she read it too late. It was because she read it too soon. She read it before she had settled in as my First Reader, as a novelist's spouse. She read it before she had learned to harness the talent, strength, advocacy, and all the skills of articulate persuasion she possessed and had—unbeknownst to her or anyone—been cultivating all her life as a passionate and opinionated devourer of novels. She didn't even really know, yet, that you could just get in there and hack a lousy novel all to pieces with a red pencil, and that—once he was through cursing and refuting and denying you—your novelist would actually thank you for having done so. *Ayelet could have saved this book,* I thought, when I had finished looking these chapters over. Maybe, someday, given time, she will. (2010)

The Mysteries of Pittsburgh

I STARTED TO WRITE *THE MYSTERIES OF PITTSBURGH* IN APRIL OF 1985, in Ralph's room. Ralph was the Christian name of a man I never met, the previous owner of my mother's house on Colton Drive, in the Montclair District of Oakland, California. His so-called room was in fact a crawl space, twice as long as it was wide, and it was not very wide. It had a cement floor and a naked lightbulb. It smelled like dirt, though not in a bad way—like soil, and cold dust, and bicycle grease. Most people would have used it for suitcases and tire chains and the lawn darts set, but at some point this Ralph had built himself a big, high, bulky workbench in there. He built it of plywood and four-by-fours, with a surface that came level to the waist of a tall man standing. It might have been a fine workbench, but it made a lousy desk, which is how I used it.

I was living with my mother and my stepfather that spring, working as an assistant in my stepfather's optometry office and trying to get the hang of California. I had moved from Pittsburgh in December with the intention of applying to an MFA program

out here. At the University of Pittsburgh I'd had three great writing teachers—Dennis Bartel, Eve Shelnutt, and Chuck Kinder—
and of them Bartel had an MFA from UC Irvine, and Kinder had
studied writing at Stanford. Both gentlemen had said they would
put in a good word for me at their respective alma maters. I'm sure
Kinder did his best, but his effort could not avail, and in the end I
found myself headed to UCI.

That winter I had been down to check out Irvine, whose writing program was staffed by a couple of novelists, Oakley Hall and
MacDonald Harris. Of the seven first-year MFA candidates I met
during my brief visit—they would of course be second-years when I
showed up the next fall—all were at work on novels (three of which,
by my count, were subsequently published—a pretty high rate). I
rode the ferry and ate a frozen banana at Balboa Island, and looked
at the ocean, and wondered if Southern California would ever feel
less strange to me, less of a place where people I would never know
led lives I couldn't imagine, than Northern California did. There
were lots of young women walking around in swimsuits and neg-
ligibly short pants and I suppose I probably wondered how many
of them I would never get to sleep with. I was kind of on a losing
streak with women at the time. I was in a bad way, actually. I was
lonely and homesick. I missed Pittsburgh. I missed the friends I
had made there, friends of whom I felt, with what strikes me now
as a fair amount of drama-queenliness, that (1) I would never see
them again on this side of the River Styx and (2) that they were in-
dissolubly bound to me by chains of fire. My loneliness and home-
sickness were of intense interest to me at the time, as were young
women in short pants, and novels, and my eternal-yet-forever-lost
friendships, and when I read a page of *Remembrance of Things Past* (as
it was then known), the book that was my project for the year, I
felt all those interests mesh, like teeth in a cog, with the teeth of

Grammar and Style, and I would imagine myself, spasmodically, a writer. I hope you can infer from the above description that I was not yet twenty-two years old.

I returned to chill gray Oakland from sunny Orange County, to the little basement room in my mother's house where I did some of my finest feeling lonely and homesick. There I ventured through a few more pages of *Swann's Way* and fretted about all those people I was soon going to be surrounded and taught by, people who were and knew themselves to be proud practitioners of novelism. Was everyone obliged to write a novel? Could I write a novel? Did I want to write a novel? What the hell was a novel, anyway, when you came right down to it? A really, really, really long short story? I hoped so, because that was the only thing I knew for certain that I could manage, sort of, to write.

Now here I was, basically required by law apparently, to start writing a goddamned novel, just because all of these windy people down at Irvine were unable to contain themselves. What kind of novel would I write? Had the time come to leave my current writing self behind?

The truth was that I had come to a rough patch in my understanding of what I wanted my writing to be. I was in a state of confusion. Over the past four years I had been struggling to find a way to accommodate my taste for the fiction I had been reading with the greatest pleasure for the better part of my life—fantasy, horror, crime, and science fiction—to the way that I had come to feel about the English language, which was that it and I seemed to have something going. Something (on my side at least) much closer to deep, passionate, physical, and intellectual love than anything else I had ever experienced with a human up to that point. But when it came to the use of language, somehow, my verbal ambition and my ability felt hard to frame or fulfill within the context of traditional genre fiction. I had found some writers, such as J. G. Ballard, Italo Calvino, J. L. Borges, and Donald Barthelme, who wrote at the critical point of language, where vapor turns to starry plasma, and yet who worked, at least sometimes, in the terms and tropes of genre fiction. They all paid a price, however. The finer and more masterly their play with language, the less connected to the conventions of traditional, bourgeois narrative form—unified point of view, coherent causal sequence of events, linear structure, naturalistic presentation—their fiction seemed to become. Duly I had written my share of pseudo-Ballard, quasi-Calvino, and neo-Borges. I had fun doing it. But no matter how hard I tried, I couldn't stop preferring the traditional, bourgeois narrative form.

I wanted to tell stories, the kind with set pieces and long descriptive passages, and "round" characters, and beginnings and middles and ends. And I wanted to instill—or rather I didn't want to *lose*—that quality, inherent in the best science fiction, which was sometimes called "the sense of wonder." If my subject matter couldn't do it—if I wasn't writing about people who sailed through neutron stars or harnessed suns together—then it was going to fall to my sentences themselves to open up the heads of my readers and decant into them enough crackling plasma to light up the eye sockets for a week. But I didn't want to *write* science fiction, or a version of science fiction, some kind of pierced-and-tattooed, doctorate-holding, ironical stepchild of science fiction. I wanted to write something with reach. Welty and Faulkner started and ended in small towns in Mississippi but somehow managed to plant flags at the end of time and in the minds of readers around the world. A good science fiction novel appeared to have an infinite reach—it could take you to the place where the universe bent back on itself— but somehow, in the end, it ended up being the shared passion of just you and that guy at the Record Graveyard on Forbes Avenue who was really into Hawkwind. I wasn't considering any actual, numerical readership here—I wasn't so bold. Rather I was thinking about the set of axioms that speculative fiction assumed, and how it was a set that seemed to narrow and refine and program its audience, like a protein that coded for a certain suite of traits. Most science fiction seemed to be written for people who already liked science fiction; I wanted to write stories for anyone, anywhere, living at any time in the history of the world. (Twenty-two, I was twenty-two!)

I paced around my room in the basement, back and forth past the bookcase where my stepfather kept the books he had bought and read in his own college days. All right, I told myself, take the practical side of things for a moment. Let's say that I did write a novel. Your basic, old-fashioned, here-and-now novel. Where would I write it? Novels took time, I assumed. They must require long hours of uninterrupted work. I needed a place where I could set up my computer, and spread out, and get my daily work done without distraction: Ralph's room. It had served Ralph as a room of his own; perhaps it would also serve me.

I lugged my computer in there and up onto the workbench. It was an Osborne 1a. I had bought it in 1983 for all that was left of my bar mitzvah money plus everything I had managed to save since. It was the size of a portable sewing machine in its molded plastic case, with two five-and-a-quarter-inch floppy disk drives, no hard drive, and 64KB of memory. At twenty-five pounds you could shlep it onto an airplane and it would just barely fit under the seat in front of you. Its screen was glowing green and slightly smaller than a three-by-five index card. It ran the CP/M operating system and had come bundled with a fine word processing program called WordStar. It never crashed, and it never failed, and I loved it immoderately. But when I hoisted it onto the surface of Ralph's workbench, and opened up one of the folding chairs that my mother stored in the crawl space, and sat down, I found that I could not reach its keys. Even standing up I could not reach the computer's fold-down keyboard without bending my forearms into contorted penguin flappers. So I dragged over the black steamer trunk my aunt Gail had bequeathed to me at some point in her wanderings and set the folding chair on top of it. The four rubber caps of the chair's steel legs fit on the trunk's lid with absurd precision, without half an inch to spare at any corner. Then I mounted the chair. I fell off. I repositioned it, and mounted it again more gingerly. I found that if I held very still, typed very chastely, and never, ever, rocked back and forth, I would be fine. Now I just needed to figure out what novel I was going to write.

I went back out to my room and shambled irritably back and forth from the door that led to the hot tub to the door that went upstairs, mapping out the confines of my skull like the bear at the Pittsburgh zoo. And my eye lighted on a relic of my stepfather's time at BU: *The Great Gatsby*.

The Great Gatsby had been the favorite novel of one of those aforementioned friends whom I had decided that, for reasons of emotional grandeur and self-poignance, I was doomed never to meet up with again in this vale of tears. At his urging I had read it a couple of years earlier, without incident or effect. Now I had the sudden intuition that if I read it again, right now, this minute, something important might result: it might change my life. Or maybe there would be something in it that I could steal.

I lay on the bed, opened its cracked paper covers—it was an old Scribner trade paperback, the edition whose cover looked like it might have been one of old Ralph's wood shop projects—and this time *The Great Gatsby* read *me*. The mythographic cast of my mind in that era, the ideas of friendship and self-invention and problematic women, the sense, invoked so thrillingly in the book's closing paragraphs, that the small, at times tawdry love-sex-and-violence story of a few people could rehearse the entire history of the United States of America from its founding vision to the Black Sox scandal—*The Great Gatsby* did what every necessary piece of fiction does as you pass though that fruitful phase of your writing life: made me want to do something just like it.

I began to detect the germ of *The Mysteries of Pittsburgh* as I finished Fitzgerald's masterpiece: I would write a novel about friendship and its impossibility, about self-inventors and dreamers of giant dreams, about problematic women and the men who make them that way. I put it back in its place on the shelf and as I did so I noticed its immediate neighbor: an old Meridian Books paperback edition of *Goodbye, Columbus* by Philip Roth, the one with the lipstick-print-and-curly-script cover art by Paul Bacon. I had never read *Goodbye, Columbus*, and as I got back into bed with it I remarked, in its lyric and conversational style, its evocation of an Eastern summer, its consciously hyperbolic presentation of the mythic Brenda Patimkin and her family of healthy, dumb, fruit-eating Jews, and its drawing of large American conclusions from small socio-erotic situations, how influenced Roth had clearly been by his own youthful reading of the Fitzgerald novel. That gave me encouragement; it made me feel as if I were preparing to sail to Cathay along a route that had already proven passable and profitable for others.

There were two more crucial observations that came out of my reading of *Goodbye, Columbus* on the heels of *The Great Gatsby*. One was that Roth's book was a hell of a lot funnier than Fitzgerald's, which almost isn't funny at all, especially when, as in the famous Party-Guest Catalog, it tries its hardest to amuse. The second observation, of the most striking parallel between the two books, got me so excited, once I noticed it, that I rushed through the whole

Mrs. Patimkin-finds-the-diaphragm sequence, so that I could get up again and resume my caged-bear perambulations: both books, I noticed, coincided precisely with a summer.

This was a parallel both deeply resonant and lastingly useful. I had just been through, in the years preceding my decampment for the West, a pair of summers that had rattled my nerves and rocked my soul and shook my sense of self—but in a good way. I had drunk a lot, and smoked a lot, and listened to a ton of great music, and talked way too much about all of those activities, and about talking about those activities. I had slept with one man whom I loved, and learned to love another man so much that it would never have occurred to me to want to sleep with him. I had seen things and gone places, in and around Pittsburgh, during those summers, that had shocked the innocent, pale, freckled Fitzgerald who lived in the great blank Minnesota of my heart.

So there was that. At the same time, the act of shaping a novel, as Fitzgerald and Roth had done, around a summer, provided an inherent dramatic structure in three acts:

I.   June.
II. July.
III. August.

Each of those months had a different purpose and a distinctive nature in my mind, and in their irrevocable order they enacted a story that always began with a comedy of expectation and ended with tragedy of remorse. All I would need to do was start at the beginning of June with high hopes and high-flying diction, and then work my way through the sex, drugs, and rock and roll to get to the oboes and bassoons of Labor Day weekend. And then maybe I would find some way, magically really, to say something about summer, about the idea of summer in America, something that great American poets of summertime like Ray Bradbury and Bruce Springsteen would have understood. Maybe, or maybe not. But at least I would be practicing the cardinal virtue that my teachers had so assiduously instilled: I would be writing about what I knew. No—I would be doing something finer than that. I would be writing about what I had known, once, but had since, in my sad and delectable state of fallenness, come to view as illusory.

I put Roth's book back on the shelf and went into Ralph's room and shut the door. I switched on the computer with its crackling little 4 MHz Zilog Z80A processor. I was cranked on summertime and the memory of summertime, on the friends who had worked so hard to become legends, on the records we listened to and the mistakes we made and the kind and mean things we did to one another. I slid a floppy disk into drive B. I paused. Was this really the kind of writer I was going to become? A writer under the influence of Fitzgerald and Roth, of books that took place in cities like Pittsburgh where people took moral instruction from the songs of Adam and the Ants? What about that sequence of stories I'd been planning about the astronomer Percival Lowell exploring the canals of Mars? What about the plan to do for romantic relationships what Calvino had done for the *urbis* in *Invisible Cities*? What about that famous sense of wonder, my animating principle, my motto and manual and standard m.o.? Was there room for that, the chance of that, along the banks of the Monongahela River? I took a deep breath, saw that I was properly balanced on my perch, and started to write—on a screen so small that you had to toggle two keys to see the end of every line—the passage that became this:

> It's the beginning of the summer and I'm standing in the
> lobby of a thousand-story grand hotel, where a bank of eleva-

tors a mile long and an endless red row of monkey attendants
in gold braid wait to carry me up, up, up, through the suites
of moguls, of spies, and of starlets; to rush me straight to the
zeppelin mooring at the art deco summit where they keep
the huge dirigible of August tied up and bobbing in the high
winds. On the way to the shining needle at the top I will wear
a lot of neckties, I will buy five or six works of genius on 45
rpm, and perhaps too many times I will find myself looking at
the snapped spine of a lemon wedge at the bottom of a drink.

I went on in this vein for several paragraphs, and some of what
I wrote that first session ended up, after much revision, at the end
of the novel, which I reached in the mid-winter of 1987, in the back
bedroom of a little house on Anade Avenue, on the Balboa Penin-
sula, shortly before my twenty-fourth birthday. At some point that
first evening, as with the help of Ralph's ghost, or of the muse who
first made her presence known to me, there, in that room under
the ground, with its smell of earth and old valises, I invoked the
spirit and the feel and the groove of summers past, I did something
foolish: I started rocking in my chair. Just a little bit, but it was too
much. I rocked backward, and fell off the trunk, and hit my head
on a steel shelf, and made a lot of noise. There was so much racket
that my mother came to the top of the stairs and called out to ask if
I was all right, and anyway, what was I doing down there?

I clambered back up from the floor, palpating the tender knot
on my skull where the angel of writers, by way of warning welcome
or harsh blessing, had just given me a mighty *zetz*. I hit the combination of keys that meant *Save*.

"I'm writing a novel," I told her. (2005)

Gentlemen of the Road

T HE ORIGINAL, WORKING—AND IN MY HEART THE TRUE—
title of the short novel you hold in your hands was *Jews With Swords*.

When I was writing it, and happened to tell people the name
of my work in progress, it made them want to laugh. I guess it
seemed clear that I meant the title as a joke. It has been a very long
time, after all, since Jews anywhere in the world routinely wore or
wielded swords, so long that when paired with "sword" the word
"Jews" (unlike say "Englishmen" or "Arabs") clangs with anachronism, with humorous incongruity, like *Samurai Tailor* or *Santa Claus
Conquers the Martians*. True, Jewish soldiers fought in the blade-era
battles of Austerlitz and Gettysburg; notoriously, Jewish boys were
stolen from their families and conscripted into the Czarist armies
of nineteenth-century Russia. Any of those fighting men, or any of
the Jews who served in the armed forces, particularly the cavalry
units, of their homelands prior to the end of WWI might have
qualified, I suppose, as Jews with swords.

But hearing the title, nobody seemed to flash on the image of

doomed Jewish troopers at Inkerman, Antietam, or the Somme, or
of dueling Arabized courtiers at Muslim Granada, or even, say, on
the memory of some ancient warrior Jew like Bar Kokhba or Ju-
dah Maccabee, famed for his prowess at arms. They saw, rather, an
unprepossessing little guy, with spectacles and a beard, brandishing
a sabre: the pirate Mottel Kamzoil. They pictured Woody Allen
backing toward the nearest exit behind a barrage of wisecracks and
a wavering rapier. They saw their uncle Manny, dirk between his
teeth, slacks belted at the armpits, dropping from the chandelier to
knock together the heads of a couple of nefarious auditors.

And, okay, so maybe I didn't look very serious when I told people my title. Yet I meant it sincerely, or half-sincerely; or maybe it
would be more accurate to say that I could not have entitled this
book any more honestly than by means of anachronism and incongruity.

I know it still seems incongruous, first of all, for me or a writer
of my literary training, generation, and pretensions to be writing
stories featuring *anybody* with swords. As recently as ten years ago
I had published two novels, and perhaps as many as twenty short
stories, and not one of them featured weaponry more antique than
a (lone) Glock 9mm. None was set any earlier than about 1972
or in any locale more far-flung or exotic than a radio studio in
Paris, France. Most of those stories appeared in sedate, respectable
and generally sword-free places like *The New Yorker* and *Harper's*,
and featured unarmed Americans undergoing the eternal fates of
contemporary short story characters—disappointment, misfortune,
loss, hard enlightenment, moments of bleak grace. Divorce; death;
illness; violence random and domestic; divorce; bad faith; deception
and self-deception; love and hate among fathers and sons, men and
women, friends and lovers; the transience of beauty and desire;
divorce—I guess that about covers it. Story, more or less, of my life.

As for the two novels, they didn't stray in time or space any farther than the stories—or for that matter, any deeper into the realm of Jewishness: both set in Pittsburgh, liberally furnished with Pontiacs and Fords, scented with marijuana, Shalimar, and kielbasa, featuring Smokey Robinson hits and *Star Trek* references, and starring gentiles or assimilated Jews, many of whom were self-consciously inspired, instructed, and laid low by the teachings of rock and roll and Hollywood but not, for example, by the lost writings of the *tzaddík* of Regensburg, whose commentaries are so important to one of the heroes of *Gentlemen of the Road*.

I'm not saying—let me be clear about this—I am not saying that I disparage, or repudiate my early work, or the genre (late-century naturalism) it mostly exemplifies. I am proud of stories like "House Hunting," "S Angel," "Werewolves in Their Youth," and "Son of the Wolfman," and out of all my novels I may always be most fond of *Wonder Boys*, which saved my life, kind of, or saved me, at least, from having to live in a world in which I must forever be held to account for the doomed second novel it supplanted. I'm not turning my back on the stuff I wrote there, late in the twentieth century, and I hope that readers won't either. It's just that here in *Gentleman of the Road* as in some of its recent predecessors you catch me in the act of trying, as a writer, to do what many of the characters in my earlier stories—Art Bechstein, Grady Tripp, Ira Wiseman—were trying, longing, ready to do: I have gone off in search of a little adventure.

If this impulse seems an incongruous thing in a writer of the ("serious," "literary") kind for which I had for a long time hoped to be taken, it might be explained—as I think the enduring popularity of all adventure fiction might be explained—with simple reference to the kind of *person* I am. I have never swung a battle-axe, or a sword. I have never, thank God, killed anybody. I have never served as a soldier of empire or fortune, infiltrated a palace or an enemy

camp in the dead of night, or ridden an elephant, though I have—
barely, and without the least confidence or style—ridden a horse.
I do not laugh in the face of death and danger—far from it. I have
never survived in the desert on a few swallows of acrid water and a
handful of scorched millet. Never escaped from prison, the gallows,
or the rowing benches of a swift caravel. Never gambled my life and
fortune on a single roll of the dice; if I lose a hundred dollars at a
Las Vegas craps table, it makes me feel like crying.

   This is not to say that I have never had adventures: I have had
my fill and more of them. Because adventures befall the unadven-
turesome as readily, if not as frequently, as the bold. Adventures are
a logical and reliable result—and have been since at least the time
of Odysseus—of the fatal act of leaving one's home, or trying to
return to it again. All adventure happens in that damned and magical space, wherever it may be found or chanced upon, which least
resembles one's home. As soon as you have crossed your doorstep or
the county line, into that place where the structures, laws, and conventions of your upbringing no longer apply, where the support and
approval (but also the disapproval and repression) of your family
and neighbors are not to be had: then you have entered into adventure, a place of sorrow, marvels, and regret. Given a choice I very
much prefer to stay home, where I may safely encounter adventure
in the pages of a book, or seek it out, as I have here, at the keyboard,
in the friendly wilderness of my computer screen.

   I guess what I'm trying to say is that if there is incongruity in
the writer of a piece of typical *New Yorker* marital-discord fare like
"That Was Me" (a story in my second collection) turning out a
swords-and-horses tale like this one, it's nothing compared to the
incongruous bounty to be harvested from the actual sight of me
sitting on a horse, for example, or trying to keep from falling out of
a whitewater raft, or setting off, as I have done from time to time

with sinking heart and in certainty of failure but goaded into wild hopefulness by some treacherous friend or bold stranger, in search of a Springsteenian something in the night.

This incongruity of writer and work suggests, of course, that classic variant of the adventure story (found in works as diverse as *Don Quixote* and *Romancing the Stone*) in which a devoted reader or author of the stuff is granted the opportunity (or obliged) to live out an adventure "in real life." And it is seen in this light that the association of Jews with swords, of Jews with adventure, may seem paradoxically less incongruous. In the relation of the Jews to the land of their origin, in the ever-extending, ever-thinning cord, braided from the freedom of the wanderer and the bondage of exile, that binds a Jew to his Home, we can make out the unmistakable signature of adventure. The story of the Jews centers around— one might almost say that it *stars*—the hazards and accidents, the misfortunes and disasters, the feats of inspiration, the travail and despair and intermittent moments of glory and grace that entail upon journeys from home and back again. For better and worse it has been one long adventure—a five-thousand-year Odyssey— from the moment of the true First Commandment, when God told Abraham *lech lecha:* Thou shalt leave home. Thou shalt get lost. Thou shalt find slander, oppression, opportunity, escape, and destruction. Thou shalt, by definition, find adventure. This long, long tradition of Jewish adventure may look a bit light on the Conans or D'Artagnans, our greatest heroes less obviously suited to exploits of derring-do and arms. But maybe that ill-suitedness only makes Jews all the more ripe to feature in (or to write) this kind of tale. Or maybe it is time to take a look backward at that tradition, as I have attempted to do here, and find some shadowy kingdom where a self-respecting Jewish adventurer would not be caught dead without his sword or his battle-axe.

And if you still think there's something funny in the idea of Jews with swords, look at yourself, right now: sitting in your seat on a jet airplane, let's say, in your unearthly orange polyester and neoprene shoes, listening to digital music, crawling across the sky from Charlotte to Las Vegas, and hoping to lose yourself—your home, your certainties, the borders and barriers of your life—by means of a bundle of wood pulp, sewn and glued and stained with blobs of pigment and resin. *People with Books*. What, in 2007, could be more incongruous than that? It makes me want to laugh. (2007)

The Phantom Tollbooth, Norton Juster

WHEN I WAS A BOY I READ, IN A BIOGRAPHY OF DANIEL Boone, or of Daniel Beard, that young Dan (whichever of the two it may have been—or maybe it was young George Washington) had so loved some book, had felt his heart and mind inscribed so deeply in its every line, that he had pricked his fingertip with a knife and, using a pen nib and his blood for ink, penned his name on the flyleaf. At once, reading that, I knew two things: (1) I must at once undertake the same procedure and (2) only one, among all the books I adored and treasured, was worthy of such tribute: *The Phantom Tollbooth*. At that point I had read it at least five or six times.

First published in 1961, *The Phantom Tollbooth* describes the epic journey of a boy named Milo, riding in a toy car, through the Kingdom of Wisdom. Along the way, Milo's journey, at first undertaken with a shrug, transforms itself into a quest, one that takes him from Expectations, through Dictionopolis, Digitopolis, and the Mountains of Ignorance, to the Castle in the Air, where a pair of princesses, Rhyme and Reason, languish in captivity. Clearly the geography and topography of the Kingdom of Wisdom, like the plot of the novel, emit a powerful whiff of the allegorical; yet somehow, through the wit and artistry and recursive playfulness of its author, Norton Juster, *The Phantom Tollbooth* manages to surmount the insurmountable obstacle that allegory ordinarily presents to pleasure.

The book appeared in my life as mysteriously as the titular tollbooth itself, brought to our house one night as a gift for me by some old friend of my father's whom I had never met before, and never saw again. Maybe all wondrous books appear in our lives the way Milo's tollbooth appears, an inexplicable gift, cast up by some curious chance that comes to feel, after we have finished and fallen in love with the book, like the workings of a secret purpose. Of all the enchantments of a beloved book the most mysterious—the most *phantasmal*—is the way they always seem to come our way precisely when we need them.

This was, I'm guessing, somewhere around 1971 (as long ago now as the days of Zeppelins, iron lungs, and Orphan Annie to me at eight years old). I was not as discontented with or disappointed by life as Milo (not yet), and I can remember feeling a faint initial disapproval of the book's mopey young protagonist the first time I read it. Life and the world still held considerable novelty and mystery for me at that time, even when strongly flavored with routine. It was hard for me to sympathize with Milo, wanting to be home when he was at school and at school when he was home. The only place I ever truly longed to be that was not where I happened to find myself (not counting dentists' chairs and Saturday-morning synagogue services) was inside the pages of a book. And here, again, as I found on finishing the novel, *The Phantom Tollbooth* understood me. Milo's journey into the Lands Beyond (beyond the flyleaf, that is, with its spectacular Jules Feiffer map) was mine as a reader, and my journey was his, and ours was the journey of all readers venturing into wonderful books, into a world made entirely, like Juster's, of language, by language, about language. While you were there, everything seemed fraught and new and notable, and when you returned, even if you didn't suffer from Milovian ennui, the "real world" seemed deeper, richer, at once *explained* and, paradoxically, more mysterious than ever. On his return from the Kingdom of Wisdom, Milo looks outside his window and finds that

> there was so much to see, and hear, and touch—walks to take, hills to climb, caterpillars to watch as they strolled through the garden [. . .] And, in the very room in which he sat, there were books that could take you anywhere, and things to invent, and make, and build, and break, and all the puzzle and excitement of everything he didn't know—music to play, songs to sing, and worlds to imagine and then someday make real.

I had wanted, carrying my sugar pills and plastic stethoscope around in a plastic black bag, to be a doctor, and then, feeling the first pangs of world-making hunger, an architect. It was while reading *The Phantom Tollbooth* that I began to realize, not that I wanted to be a writer (that came a little later, at the mercy of Sir Arthur Conan Doyle), but something simpler: I had a crush on the English language, one that was every bit as intense, if less advanced, as that from which the augustly named Mr. Norton Juster himself evidently suffered.

I am the son and grandson of helpless, hardcore, inveterate punsters, and when I got to Milo getting lost in The Doldrums where he found a (strictly analog) watchdog named Tock, it was probably already too late for me. I was gone on the book, riddled like a body in a cross fire by its ceaseless barrage of wordplay—the arbitrary and diminutive apparatchik, Short Shrift; the kindly and feckless witch, Faintly Macabre; the posturing Humbug; and, of course, the Island of Conclusions, reachable only by jumping.

Puns—the word's origin, like the name of some pagan god, remains unexplained by etymologists—are derided, booed, apologized for. When my father and grandfather committed acts of punmanship they were often, generally by the women at the table or in the car with them, begged if not ordered to cease at once. "Every time I see you," my grandfather liked to tell me, grinning, during the days of my growth spurt, "you grusomer!" Maybe puns are a guy thing; I don't know. I can't see how anybody who claims to love language can't fail to marvel at the beautiful slipperiness of meaning that puns, like aquarium nets, momentarily catch and bring shimmering to the surface. Puns act to shatter or at least compromise meaning; a pun condenses unrelated, even opposing meanings, like a collapsing dwarf star, into a singularity. Maybe it's this anti-semantic vandalism that leads so many people to shun and revile them.

And yet I would argue—and it's a lesson I learned first from my grandfather and father and then in the pages of *The Phantom Tollbooth*—that puns, in fact, operate to generate new meanings, outside and beyond themselves. Anyone who jumps to conclusions, as to Conclusions, is liable to find himself isolated, alone, unable to reconnect easily with the former texture and personages of his life. Without the punning island first charted by Norton Juster, we might not understand the full importance of maintaining a cautionary distance toward the act of jumping to conclusions, as Mr. Juster implicitly recommends.

But it was not just the puns and wordplay that gave me a bad case of loving English. It was the words themselves: the vocabulary of the book. I can still, forty years later, remember my first encounters with the following words: macabre, din, dodecahedron, discord, trivium, lethargy. They are all, capitalized and adapted, characters in the novel. Entire phrases, too, found their way into the marbles sack of my eight-year-old word-hoard: "rhyme and reason," "easy as falling off a log," "taking the words right out of your mouth." To this day when I happen to write those or any other of the words that I remember having first seen in *The Phantom Tollbooth*, I get a tiny thrill of nostalgia and affection for the wonderful book, and for its author, and for myself when young, and for the world I then lived in. A world of wonders, but not so replete that it could not be improved upon, perhaps even healed, by a journey like Milo's, through a book. But if you've read the book, you probably know what I'm talking about. If you haven't, what are you doing at the afterword? Stop reading this nonsense, already, and go back to Chapter 1. I'll be waiting here for you, with a pin to prick your fingertip. (2011)

Wonder When You'll Miss Me, Amanda Davis

Only dead writers get afterwords. Among all the hateful consequences of the early death of Amanda Davis, on March 14, 2003, both to those who loved and miss her and to lovers of contemporary American fiction, this particular one—the words that you are now reading—is probably the most minor. I have spent the past five months or so hating every thing, and there have been so many, that has come along, or popped up, or appeared in a magazine or the day's mail, to remind me that Amanda is dead. And now here I am, creating my own black-edged reminder. I guess that it's a cliché to write "it saddens me to have to write these words," but if so, the sentiment expressed is one that I have never truly experienced in my life before now. Every word that I string along here is bringing a cliché lump to my throat and a cliché tear to my eye. Every one of them is like each day that has passed since the fourteenth of March, a wedge driven into the crack that opened that afternoon, leaving Amanda forever on her side, back there, in the world that had Amanda Davis in it. There was no place, no need, in that world, for an afterword.

My wife, Ayelet Waldman, met her before I did—roped by Amanda and her golden lasso into a friendship that while heartbreakingly brief was one of the truest and fiercest I have ever stood next to and admired—and one of the first things she told me about Amanda is, I think, the most germane to my purpose here. "I just finished her book," Ayelet said, referring to the novel that you, too, have presumably just finished reading. "*She's the real thing.*" Or maybe what she said was "*The girl can write.*" I'm not sure, anymore. It's only after your friend's airplane has crashed into a mountain in North Carolina—killing her, at the age of thirty-two, along with her mother and her father, who was flying the plane—that everything she ever said to you, and everything anyone ever said to you about her, takes on the weight and shadow, the damnable *significance*, of history.

At the time, all that really registered, when I heard about Amanda from Ayelet, was the rare note of true enthusiasm in the voice of my wife, who reads almost everything, and in particular everything by youthful female novelists, and in particular those novels that treat in some way of damaged girls with body-image problems, of which, God knows, there have been many, with doubtless many still to come. Some of these novelists, some of whose books she admired, she had also met, and liked, as she had instantly liked Amanda. Never had she pronounced this judgment on any of them. It was obvious to her that Amanda *had the goods*—maybe that was what she told me—and then, when I read Amanda's books, it was obvious to me, too. Her sentences had the quality of laws of nature, they were at once surprising and inevitable, as if Amanda had not written so much as discovered them. As the catcher Crash Davis said to his wild and talented young pitcher, Ebby LaLoosh,

"God reached down from the sky and gave you a thunderbolt for a right arm." Amanda had that kind of great stuff.

It's unfair, as well as cruel, to try to assess the overall literary merit, not to mention the prospects for future greatness, of a young woman who managed to produce (while living a life replete as a Sabatini novel with scoundrels, circus performers, sterling friendships, true love, hair's-breadth escapes, jobs at once menial and strange, and years of hard rowing in the galleys of the publishing world) a single short story collection, the remarkable *Circling the Drain*, and a lone novel. I would give a good deal of money, blood, books, or years to be able to watch as Amanda, in a picture hat, looked back from the vantage of a long and productive career to reject her first published efforts as uneven, or "only halfway there," or, worst of all, as *promising*; or to see her condescend to them, cuddle them almost, as mature writers sometimes do with their early books, the way we give our old stuffed pony or elephant, with its one missing shirt-button eye, a fond squeeze before returning it to the hatbox in the attic.

At bottom of this kind of behavior on the part of old, established writers is the undeniable way in which our young selves, and the books that issued from them, invariably seem to reproach us: with the fading of our fire, the diminishment of our porousness to the world and the people in it, the compromises made, the friendships abandoned, the opportunities squandered, the loss of velocity on our fastball. But Amanda never got to live long enough to sense the presence of her fine short stories and of this stirring, charming, beautifully written novel, as any kind of a threat or reproof. She was merely, justly proud of them. On some level that was not buried very deeply, she *knew* that she was the real thing. This is, in fact, a characteristic of writers who are (alas it is often found, as well, among those who are not). After *Wonder When You'll Miss Me,* she was going to write a historical novel about early Jewish immigrants to the South, or a creepy modern gothic, and then after that she was going to try any one of a hundred other different kinds of novels, because she felt, rightly, that with her command of the English language, and her sharp, sharp mind, and her omnivorous interests, and her understanding of human emotion, and, above all, with her unstoppable, inevitable, tormenting, at times even *unwelcome,* compulsion to do the work, the hard and tedious work, she could have written just about any book she damn well wanted to.

And we will never get to read any of them. This and the story collection are all that we have, and the crack in the world falls farther and farther behind us. And Amanda's there, and we're here, and I've never yet written or read a book, with or without an afterword, that could do anything at all about that. (2004)

APPENDIX: LINER NOTES

1980–1996, Carsickness

I saw Carsickness play for the first time in the fall of 1980, somewhere on the campus of Carnegie-Mellon University, where I was a freshman; it might have been in the old Skibo Ballroom.

I had listened to their self-released EP about a hundred and seven times by then, and I thought their live show was very exciting. There was nothing very exciting, however, about the five guys who made up the band. They had on jeans, T-shirts, sneakers. One of them wore a cardigan sweater. A couple of the guys verged, particularly when it came to the way they wore their hair, on the unkempt, but most of them looked, frankly, a lot like CMU engineering students. None looked even remotely, in the fall of 1980, like punks. This came very much as a relief to me, I remember. I was kind of afraid of punks, or at any rate I was going to be afraid of them, I believed, if I ever actually met any. They did not have punks in the suburban Maryland town where I had grown up and bought my first Clash, Blondie, and Jam records.

I had been introduced to the music of Carsickness shortly after arriving at CMU by a dude on my dormitory hall (Donner A-Level West) who was the first, but by no means the last, ninth-level grandmaster of rock fandom I ever met. His name was John Fetkovich, but people called him Fetko. His knowledge was deep, wide, and intricately hyperlinked. He could steer you from the Velvet Underground to David Bowie to Uriah Heep to Pere Ubu to Patti Smith to Bruce Springsteen in one listening session without ever departing his zone of musical happiness. He was an engineering major, bespectacled, small of stature, and generous with his knowledge and with the contents of his record collection. He had a slot on WRCT, the campus radio station, and in time became a vigorous local champion of bands that had begun to ooze and bubble up from dark subterranean seams all over America: Hüsker Dü, X, Black Flag, the Minutemen, the Meat Puppets, etc. He spoke in brief, precise declaratives, with a Jim Henson gulp in his voice, bobbing his head for emphasis. There was a certain air of Muppetry about Fetko.

"If you like punk," he had told me, soon—like, *minutes*—after we first met, "you should check out Carsickness." He bobbed his head. "They're from here, and they're great."

I went out and bought the aforementioned EP—it had four songs, among them the local "hit" "Bill Wilkinson" with its radio-hostile chorus—and, as I said, I loved it. But did I like *punk*? And *were* Carsickness a punk band?

They didn't look it, as I've said—no mohawks, no safety pins, not much leather in evidence—and they didn't sound it either, apart from the vocals, and the angry politics that fueled most of the lyrics. Leader and lead singer Joe Soap (a pseudonymous Irish immigrant, it was said, whose precarious status was reflected in another song on that EP, "Illegal Alien") often sounded a lot like

Joe Strummer at his most drunken, if you know what I mean—the plaintive, heartbroken Strummer of "The Right Profile" and the final 00:30 of "Hate and War."

Even a cursory listen to this disc, however, will yield very little in the way of the kind of blunt, buzzing, major-chord drums-bass-guitar attack, formulated by the Ramones and codified in the UK, that by 1980 had already become conventionalized as "punky," and none of ironic-nostalgic Sha-Na-Na-meets-Artaud pastiche vibe, Warhol's drag-queen aesthetic filtered through the New York Dolls, that characterized the sound of many of the New York punk bands. Carsickness played songs that were rhythmically complicated, sonically adventurous, and instrumentally distinctive— saxophones! guitarists who could double on keyboards!—with drummer Dennis Childers laying down tricky time signatures and the rest of the band managing very nicely, thank you, to keep up. Their songs wandered musically in and out of genres, often in the course of a single track, and the band was not afraid, now and then, in their own spiky, frustrated way, to swing. At times Carsickness seemed—to my ear, at least—to verge on jazz or even (could it be?) on prog. They made music as hyperlinked and omnivorous, as disrespectful of boundaries as the musical taste of John Fetkovich (or of any ninth-level grandmaster of rock fandom, in my experience).

In Pittsburgh, in 1980, they were playing a music that didn't yet have—and would never really find—a name: "post-punk."

In fact it might be argued that in their restlessness to move, musically if not politically, beyond the stupid-is-smart aesthetic of punk, Carsickness *invented* post-punk—in Pittsburgh. Just as Hüsker Dü and Gang of Four and Mission of Burma and Sonic Youth were busy restlessly inventing it in Minneapolis, London, Boston, and New York. Just as, a few years later, bands in Pittsburgh that were made up of post-post-punks like me and my friends, kids who loved the Birthday Party and Wire but refused to stop listening to their Black Sabbath records, would spontaneously evolve a kind of heavy, heavy music that was called—as we would in time be informed by a Seattle-obsessed national media—"grunge." (Moral of the story of Pittsburgh rock 'n' roll, over and over and over again: if you want musical immortality, move somewhere else.)

I didn't know, in the fall of 1980, that there was something called "post-punk." But I could tell—anybody could tell—that Carsickness were moving in another direction. They had pulled up stakes and struck out for some hinterland beyond the kingdom of punk. Even thirty-five (good lord!) years later, you can still hear it in the songs on this record: the sound of five young men united, for a time, by a sense of adventure. It's the sound of my youth—and yours, whenever you were born, wherever you came of age, however you came into possession of the restlessness that is our common inheritance. (2017)

Uptown Special Vinyl Edition, Mark Ronson

INTRODUCTION

"I don't really know where the title came from. It was just something people said, just a term we used. Like, when you don't see somebody around for a bit, when they've sort of gone missing, socially. You say, so-and-so 'moved uptown' or, you know, 'he's riding the Uptown Special.'"
MARK RONSON (TO THE BEST OF MY RECOLLECTION),
LONDON, JANUARY 2014

IF YOU'RE READING THESE NOTES—IF YOU TAKE ENOUGH OF an interest in Mark Ronson and his music to dig so deep into the sofa cushions, feeling around for one last shiny dime—then by now you've probably heard the story. It's the conventional wisdom, part

of the mythology of this record: the story of Ronson's so-called
lost or uptown years: how the scenes he made, and the beaches he
washed up on, and the sweet American music he imbibed in the
course of that strange journey became the raw material for this, his
fourth album.

Just to make it clear at the outset: as far as I know, everything you've heard or read is bullshit. There's nothing, no truth,
in any of the outrageous claims that have been put forward, by the
media and by various sketchy characters claiming to have "been
there." No Russian (or in some versions, Georgian) mobsters.
No spiritual quest in the Nevada desert or under the tutelage of
a slide-guitar-playing Delta hoodoo man. No monthlong, six-
figure blackjack benders. No desperate transcontinental pursuit
of an elusive, beautiful high-wire aerialist and "human cannon-
ball," as her circus company crisscrossed the country. All of that is
slander at worst and at best the outcome of too many people with
active imaginations getting a little too baked and then having at
it on Genius.com.

Part of the blame for this mess, and he'd be the first to admit it,
lies squarely on the shoulders of Ronson himself. He never showed
much interest in talking about the "Uptown Years" (a term that
always makes him smile), preferring, as he would patiently explain
to friends and interviewers alike, to let the music speak for itself.
Until he played these songs for me, I had never heard much from
Ronson about those years except when, for whatever reason, he
would be caught off guard by some sudden fond memory of his days
on the road as a roving ambassador for the American Automobile
Association (AAA)'s Car Safety and Care-A-Van program. I can't
say that I was surprised when I learned the truth, though. Anyone
who knows Ronson has heard his little lectures on the importance

of regularly checking tire pressure, or keeping a well-stocked emergency kit in the vehicle. Whatever the reason for Ronson's having fallen into what he prefers to call "my little uptown funk," there is nothing mysterious in the cure he hit upon: lighting out for the territory, like Huck Finn, in a well-maintained, low-mileage 1994 stretch Lincoln Town Car,* its rear seating area and capacious trunk loaded with boxes full of literature on winterizing your vehicle and not, as some have claimed, bootleg Chinese semi-automatic rifles, stolen pharmaceuticals, or (you have to love this one) an alcoholic circus bear named Julio.

With the CD-and-digital release of *Uptown Special*, however, as a seemingly endless parade of night-runners, minor dudes, and demimondaines have been dragged blinking into the light and encouraged to recount, or rather concoct, the "Shocking Truth about Ronno's Uptown Years,"† Ronson's reticence has come to seem, in hindsight, like a tactical error. As the bizarre tales and baroque inventions have proliferated, Ronson has reluctantly begun to concede that he may not have entirely succeeded in his effort, on *Uptown Special*, to get across, purely through music and lyrics, the story, the true story, of the time he spent "riding the Uptown Special."

After conducting extensive interviews with Ronson in London, and with his full cooperation and encouragement, I have prepared these liner notes. They are as accurate as I can make them, given the limitations of memory and the fact that the device I used to record

---

* Acquired, legend has it, in a trade for his Grammy statuette and a dozen pairs of limited-edition Mark Ronson Gucci sneakers. Legend, in this instance, is mistaken. I have seen the bill of sale for the car, from a New Jersey dealer specializing in sales of used livery vehicles. As for the statuette, it remains safe in its accustomed location on a credenza in Ronson's mother's living room, in Syosset, Long Island, next to a framed photo of Ronson at his bar mitzvah.

† According to a recent headline in the *Daily Mail* of London.

the interviews was afterword stolen by a man who attacked and
robbed me as I was coming out of the North Sea Fish Restaurant.*
I hope that in addition to popping certain people's crazy-balloons,
these notes will prove welcome to interested fans of Ronson's
music, some of whom no doubt recall the joy and the mystery you
used to be able to find, routinely, in the sleeve of an LP, where the
liner notes, the lyric sheet, and a thing called Meaning once played
their shy, flirtatious games.

"UPTOWN'S FIRST FINALE"

THIS BRIEF INTRODUCTION, HAUNTED EQUALLY BY STEVIE
Wonder's chromatic harmonica and the ever-present specter, in
summer weather or warm climates, of your engine overheating,
hints at the setting of track seven, "Crack in the Pearl," Ronson's
epic cautionary tale of poor maintenance leading to an unplanned
breakdown in the desert "nine exits north of Las Vegas."

"SUMMER BREAKING"

WHILE ITS TITLE MIGHT SUGGEST ANOTHER WARNING ABOUT
the threat posed to a car's engine by extreme temperatures (something Ronson feels cannot be overstated) and the need to regularly monitor vehicle fluids, "Summer Breaking" is concerned

---

* Though he did have a Russian (or, I suppose, a Georgian) accent, there is no truth
to reports that my assailant was wearing limited-edition Mark Ronson Gucci sneakers.
Lying with my face on the sidewalk, as he ran away down Leigh Street, I had ample
opportunity to observe the man's footwear, and they looked much more like boat shoes
than sneakers.

with another, more alarming automotive danger. In the spring of
2011, the "totally dope" (i.e., "hip" and/or "cool") DJ/Producer/
AAA Roving Ambassador was invited to bring his one-man Car
Safety and Care-A-Van to West Oakland, California, where he
addressed a receptive and attentive group of young people. The
topic? A bizarre and extremely hazardous "pastime" known as
"ghost-riding the whip" or simply "ghost-riding" in which partic-
ipants deliberately abandon a slowly moving vehicle in order to
dance around or even *on top* of it.* After introducing his "typical
teenager" protagonist, a young woman engaged in the kind of un-
wise practices that increase the likelihood of risky behaviors like
"ghost-riding the whip," Ronson admonishes her to "be the girl
you [. . .] pretend not to be" and "play the game" of making safe
and sensible choices.

"Feel Right"

We Americans love our cars, but in order to "feel
right," according to Ronson, it's important to get out from behind
the wheel sometimes and get some exercise. Extolling the health
benefits of bicycle riding ("It's exercise with thighs and hip muscles"), Mystikal also offers Ronson's tips on bicycle safety (a perennial concern of Ronson's music, as per his 2010 hit "The Bike
Song"), delivering a vivid reminder about the importance of always
wearing a helmet while biking in order to avoid serious head injury:
"You gon' fuck around and [. . .] knock your fruit juice loose,
banana, your watermelon and pomegranate, too."

---

* To the accompaniment, naturally, of music played at volumes injurious to their hearing.

"Uptown Funk"

Far from the bacchanalian dance floor call-to-arms it has widely been taken for, this is Ronson's heartfelt confession of the dark period, following the release of his underappreciated 2009 album "Record Collection," when he slipped into the depression that he now jokingly refers to as his "little uptown funk." In fact, during this time, Ronson was seriously "funked up." He became obsessed with the film actress Michelle Pfeiffer, suffered from repeated psychosomatic hot flashes ("Too hot!"), and shocked friends and family with his uncharacteristically disheveled and confused physical appearance, even going so far as to show up at an important function dressed in an Yves Saint Laurent suit and a pair of worn-out old canvas trainers. With the introduction, in the song's interlude, of Mr. Julio Ruiz, the AAA's Special Programs director, and with the purchase of a secondhand stretch Town Car, Ronson hints at his eventual recovery and renewed sense of purpose in life.

"I Can't Lose"

In the course of the autumn of 2011, delivering talks in cold-weather regions on proper winterization and safe driving techniques for winter weather, Ronson perfected an amusing routine focused on one of the major culprits in snow-and-ice-related traffic accidents: driver overconfidence. Between their faith in antilock brake systems and the like, and their misplaced faith in their own skill levels, many drivers feel that they "can't lose" control of their vehicle. Ronson's gentle but pointed mockery, reflected in this song (whose original opening line was reportedly

"When I drove you last night, baby/And we hit that patch of ice"), elicited many a droll chuckle and nod of recognition in the senior centers and church basements of the Midwest and Northeast.

"Daffodils"

With a clarity and a directness that really require no annotation, Ronson delivers another hard-hitting warning, this time on the dangers of mixing driving with prescription (and many over-the-counter) medications. Those who neglect manufacturers' warnings to avoid operating heavy machinery (the "kick dragon" and "vapor wagon" of the first stanza) may find themselves driving "right off the map"—and off the road!

"Crack in the Pearl"

According to Ronson, the most autobiographical track on the record, a sad account of how a long-anticipated road trip to Las Vegas was ruined by his own failure to adequately maintain his vehicle and to prepare it for prolonged exposure to intense desert heat. "I didn't flush and replace the coolant every 24,000 miles, I didn't check the water in the radiator, I didn't make sure the battery was fastened tightly in place, which cuts down on heat-generating vibrations. When we broke down, nine exits north of Las Vegas, we couldn't get all the way onto the shoulder, and I didn't even have a flare in the trunk." He paused to shake his head ruefully. "I just totally blew it, and the whole trip that was supposed to be so great turned out to be a total drag. Not at all how I laid it out for my buddy, not how he pictured it." It was a real road-to-Damascus moment for Ronson. "That's when I first started to get serious about car care and safety."

"IN CASE OF FIRE"

1. Exit the vehicle immediately.
2. If possible, turn off engine before exiting the vehicle.
3. Get as far away from the vehicle as possible.
4. Call the fire department.
5. Do not return to the car under any circumstances.

"LEAVING LOS FELIZ"

LIKE "UPTOWN FUNK," A SONG THAT REFLECTS THE MALAISE and mounting sense of something lacking from his life that led Ronson to "move uptown" and seek a renewed sense of purpose by taking time off from his transatlantic music career to reconnect with the "American highway" (from Harlem to Hollywood to Jackson, Mississipi, as "Uptown Funk" itinerizes it) and spread the gospel of sensible automotive safety and maintenance practices.

"HEAVY AND ROLLING"

THE CULMINATING MOMENT OF THE ALBUM'S JOURNEY, ITS New York City homecoming, and the thematic counterweight to "Crack in the Pearl" with its account of roadside calamity, "Heavy and Rolling" is Ronson's paean to the glories of life behind the wheel of his beloved, flawlessly maintained Town Car with its low center of gravity, rolling on tires that have been inflated according to the manufacturer's recommendation. Rarely in the history of pop music has an artist come so close to articulating the deep, quiet satisfaction of knowing one's vehicle is as ready as it can be for any and all of the potential hazards faced by drivers today. (2015)

The rest is rust and stardust.
—VLADIMIR NABOKOV

About the Author

Michael Chabon lives in Berkeley, California, with his wife, the novelist Ayelet Waldman, and their children.

PROCEEDS FROM THIS BOOK BENEFIT
THE MACDOWELL COLONY

Located in Peterborough, New Hampshire, the MacDowell Colony is a contemporary arts organization that nurtures artists in seven disciplines, fosters cultural dialogue, and expands appreciation of the arts. Awarded through an open application process, MacDowell Fellowships champion a diverse group of emerging and established artists by providing residencies on MacDowell's 450-acre property, while Edward MacDowell Medal Day and MacDowell community programs engage a wider public with the creative process. The first of its kind and the model for residency programs today, The MacDowell Colony was awarded the National Medal of Arts for inspiring many of this century's finest artists. With more than 14,500 residencies since 1907, MacDowell fuels a growing legacy of award winning artworks exhibited, published and performed around the world. The Colony depends upon public interest, concern, and generosity to continue to provide an ideal working place for exceptional artists, and it is grateful to the many who have given their support. To learn more or to apply, visit www.macdowellcolony.org. And, thank you!

Michael Chabon, a MacDowell Fellow and the chairman of MacDowell's Board of Directors since 2010, has requested that all royalties from Bookends be turned over to the MacDowell Colony in perpetuity.

ALSO BY MICHAEL CHABON

"An immensely gifted writer and magical prose stylist."
—**Michiko Kakutani**, *New York Times*

MYSTERIES OF PITTSBURGH
A Novel
Available in Paperback

A MODEL WORLD AND OTHER STORIES
Available in Paperback

THE FINAL SOLUTION
A Story of Detection
Available in Paperback, eBook, and Audiobook

THE YIDDISH POLICEMEN'S UNION
A Novel
Available in Paperback, eBook, Audiobook, and Digital Audio

MAPS AND LEGENDS
Reading and Writing Along the Borderlands
Available in Paperback

MANHOOD FOR AMATEURS
The Pleasures and Regrets of a Husband, Father, and Son
Available in Paperback, eBook, Large Print, Audiobook, and Digital Audio

TELEGRAPH AVENUE
A Novel
Available in Paperback, eBook, Large Print, Audiobook, and Digital Audio

SUMMERLAND
A Novel
Available in Paperback, eBook, Large Print, and Digital Audio

MOONGLOW
A Novel
Available in Paperback, eBook, Large Print, Audiobook, and Digital Audio

KINGDOM OF OLIVES AND ASH
Writers Confront the Occupation
Available in Paperback, eBook, and Digital Audio

POPS
Fatherhood in Pieces
Available in Hardcover, Paperback, eBook, Large Print, and Digital Audio